NEW CASTLE'S
KADUNCE
MURDERS

NEW CASTLE'S
KADUNCE
MURDERS

MYSTERY AND THE DEVIL *in*
NORTHWEST PENNSYLVANIA

DALE RICHARD PERELMAN

THE
History
PRESS

Published by The History Press
Charleston, SC
www.historypress.com

Copyright © 2019 by Dale Richard Perelman
All rights reserved

Front cover: Larry Kadunce on his way to court. *Courtesy of the New Castle Police.*

First published 2019

Manufactured in the United States

ISBN 9781467144025

Library of Congress Control Number: 2019948133

CONTENTS

NOTE ON SOURCES

The events described in this book are sourced directly from court records, police files, trial transcripts or actual interviews by the author. The writer has taken minor poetic license in describing some physical movements and emotions, although these are justified based on actual records.

TOO NICE A DAY FOR A KILLING

Robins chirped at their brothers perched on neighboring limbs. Green leaves fluttered across the maple trees. Roses bloomed vivid reds and yellows. Nikki hydrangeas added a touch of purple and blue. A bed of Stella day lilies cascaded with orange and coral hues interspersed with a clump of nearby daisies. Although the early hours still retained a chill from the night air, the day promised perfect weather later in the afternoon—ideal for a picnic at New Castle's Gaston Park, a stroll through Cascade Park or even a swim in Neshannock Creek by the Paper Mill Bridge.

The Kadunce house (to reader's right). *Author's collection.*

The morning sun glided across the sky, brightening the little rental home at 708 Wilmington Avenue, located just blocks from downtown. Kathy Kadunce lay in bed and nursed her newborn infant, Robert, nicknamed "Dino," at her breast. Daughter Dawn snuggled against her teddy bear as she slept quietly in the adjoining room. The early morning started so peacefully. The date was Tuesday, July 11, 1978, the heart of summer—far too nice a day for a murder.

ACKNOWLEDGEMENTS

This book tells the story of a brutal murder of a mother and her four-year-old daughter in the hardscrabble town of New Castle, Pennsylvania, during the summer of 1978. The saga intermingles a serial killer, a Satanist, multiple suicides, three courtroom trials and questions of innocence and guilt. All facts are true, taken from actual police documents, interviews and court records.

This book would not have been possible without the help of prothonotary Helen Morgan; District Attorney Josh Lamancusa; attorney Norman Levine; detectives Frank Gagliardo, Chuck Abraham, Matthew Vanasco and Vincent Martwinski; Police Chief Bobby Salem; Banks Smither and Abigail Fleming of The History Press; and Chris Fabian from the New Castle Public Library. My son, Sean Kanan, and my daughter, Robyn Bernstein, both highly skilled writers, along with Phil Gasiewicz, with whom I shared a summer writing class at Yale University, have provided emotional and editorial help. Lastly and most importantly, I wish to acknowledge my wife, Michele, my muse, my critic and my number-one reader.

Helen Morgan, prothonotary for thirty-eight years and sister of Frank Gagliardo. *Author's collection.*

Introduction

A TASTE OF THE TOWN

New Castle, Pennsylvania, a rustbelt town of slightly more than thirty thousand, stood fifty miles north of Pittsburgh. A hodgepodge of Italians, Poles, Syrians, Lebanese, Greeks and the occasional bearded Amish family from nearby New Wilmington driving a horse and black buggy populated the area. Many locals held blue-collar jobs in outmoded manufacturing plants like Rockwell Axle, Shenango Pottery, Pentax Foundry or Universal Rundle. Some workers traveled outside the county to nearby Sharon Steel in Mercer County or to the General Motors assembly division in Lordstown, Ohio.

Little of significance stirred up the community. Each day quietly folded into the next. Movies offered an avenue of escape. John Travolta and Olivia Newton-John rocked the Highlander Theater on the North Hill with *Grease*, bringing back the nostalgic 1950s. *The Bad News Bears* played downtown at the Cinema to younger audiences. On the South Side, X-rated movies scintillated voyeurs at the seedy State Theater.

To infuse new life into a sagging downtown, the Redevelopment Authority began to widen the sidewalks and remove the parking meters from the streets, generating temporary employment. The construction disrupted business, dampening hopes for a strong back-to-school season. The disappearance of several stately multistory buildings and their replacement single-floor utilitarian structures caused one astute merchant to compare the new construction to the exchange of fine leather for Naugahyde. The *New Castle News* urged the public to overlook this temporary inconvenience and patronize the city's shops, but sales slipped away to neighboring Youngstown, Sharon and Pittsburgh.

New Castle qualified as a sports-crazy town. During the fall season, Friday nights meant high school football. Everyone followed Coach Lindy Lauro's Red Hurricanes, one of Pennsylvania's most successful football teams. Back in 1951, Lindy had become the National Football League's oldest rookie with the old Chicago Cardinals at age twenty-nine.

In the spring and summer, local baseball legend Chuck Tanner took center stage. As a rookie outfielder with the Milwaukee Braves in 1955, Tanner blasted a home run on the first pitch during his first at bat. From 1977 to 1985, he managed the Pittsburgh Pirates. On off nights, Tanner could be found talking baseball with his cronies at Egidio's Restaurant on Wilmington Road. Tanner's warmth and enthusiasm made him everybody's friend. While the newspaper debated whether the Pirates should trade star outfielder Dave Parker for someone less outspoken and controversial, the people on the streets argued the player's pros and cons. Residents felt a proprietary interest in such a decision due to their kinship with Tanner and the Pirates.

New Castle's citizens enjoyed ethnic foods almost as much as sports. The city's restaurants offered a mouthwatering mishmash of sights, tastes and smells—the greasy aroma of fresh sausage pizza, deep-fried smelts, wedding soup thick with meatballs and escarole, the sizzle of lamb on the rod and the lure of steaming hot dogs on the grill, loaded with onions, mustard and chili. The cry of "two with everything and a side of fries" echoed through the Hudson Lunch, the Coney Island Grill and the Post Office Lunch, all owned by Greek Americans.

Large families routinely gathered together on Sundays following church in New Castle. After a late lunch or early dinner, the women washed dishes and hashed out gossip while the men argued politics or sports to the din of the television.

Cooking remained a family ritual. The Italian women, and frequently the men, labored over the stove to create a masterpiece of fresh tomato sauce brimming with meatballs, pepperoni or sausage to accompany rigatoni, penne or linguine pastas for the upcoming feast. The Poles made pierogis, mashed potatoes and sauerkraut among other favorites. Other ethnic groups cooked up their own favorite recipes.

In the mid-to-late 1970s, an influx of imported steel and pottery started to suck the economy dry. Plants began to lay off newer workers and even close. Doctors, lawyers and other professionals exited the city limits in

Coney Island hot dogs sign. *Author's collection.*

droves for newer homes and offices in suburban Neshannock Township. The younger and more mobile departed the area entirely, gravitating to major metropolitan cities. Poverty gripped the unemployed and underemployed in a vise of declining job opportunities, locking them in housing projects like Halco Drive or the Village. Facing diminished legal avenues to earn a decent living, a seamy underbelly oozed through the city. The understaffed and overburdened police eyeballed the growth of drug activity and petty thefts with growing interest, gathering evidence for future prosecution.

1

THE CRIME

Thirty-five-year-old, prematurely aging Rose Butera and her teenage daughter Lori opened the doors of a dented Cadillac after leaving the gynecologist's office around 1:15 in the afternoon. Lori's boyfriend Brian Baer waited for them in the driver's seat.

"Well at least that's over. Let's go," Rose said.

Brian headed back toward the Butera house. When he braked at the light on Taylor Street, Lori piped up, "Mom, let's stop and visit Kathy. It's almost on the way, and we'll get to see baby Dino, too. Please?" Lori flashed her broadest winning smile. Kathy Kadunce used to live on Crawford Street behind Rose and Lori's working-class home on Oak. Kathy had been Lori's babysitter when she was little. Lori thought of her as an older sister and confidante, and she occasionally babysat Kathy's four-year-old daughter, Dawn.

Rose recalled a day the previous summer when Dawn picked flowers from her yard. The child's misbehavior had embarrassed Kathy, but Rose laughed about the incident. The very next morning, Kathy replaced the missing flowers with artificial ones as a joke. Rose saw Kathy as a flower, not fully in bloom, who escaped her humdrum life in romance and science-fiction novels. Kathy loved to sew. She decorated pillowcases and designed clothing for her children. Once, she monogrammed green handbags for Rose's daughters. Since Kathy nurtured few friendships other than her mother, her sister and her sister-in-law, she frequently confided in "Mama Rose" about her troubled marriage. A few years earlier, the police had arrested Kathy's husband, Lawrence "Lou" Kadunce (also known as Larry), for indecent exposure on four separate occasions over a three-month period, costing him six weeks of jail time. Kathy feared another misstep would cost Lou his job and her a marriage.

"Sure, honey, a trip to see Kathy would be fun."

Brian turned the car around and proceeded up the North Hill. Kathy's home on Wilmington Road lay only a few blocks away from them. The Butera ladies looked forward to seeing Kathy, her cute little daughter Dawn and baby Robert, already nicknamed "Dino." Besides, the stop would distract Rose from thoughts on her recent hysterectomy and the day's doctor's appointment.

Brian parked at the rear entrance to Kathy's house. The trio ambled toward the back door, chattering along the walkway.

Rose tugged on the handle of the storm door and entered through an unlocked and partially open inner door. Odd, she thought, Kathy always locked her door. "Kathy, Rose is here," Mrs. Butera called. No answer. A crying baby, clad in a terrycloth sleeper, lay on his back in a port-a-crib. Rose picked up the infant, feeling his soaked bottom.

The rear entrance to the Kadunce home. *Author's collection.*

"What's a matter with Auntie Rose's little guy?" She rocked baby Dino to and fro in her arms. "There now, stop your crying."

"Kathy must be upstairs and can't hear us. Lori, why don't you pop upstairs and see if she and Dawn are taking a bath?"

"Sure, Mom," Lori said, bounding up the stairs to surprise Kathy and Dawn.

Within seconds, Lori emitted a piercing scream.

"What's going on up there?" Rose shouted from the dining room with the baby still in her arms.

Lori appeared on the bottom step. Her fingers strangled the railing; her other hand trembled at her side. Lori's lips quivered as she stuttered, "Mom, Mom."

"What's wrong?" Rose asked.

"Dawn's upstairs with blood all over her."

"Where?" Rose said. *Had Dawn gotten cut by one of her mother's razors?*

"In her bedroom."

"What do you mean she's got blood all over her?"

"Don't you understand? She's got blood all over her," Lori yelped. She released her hold on the bannister and gesticulated wildly.

"Did you see Kathy?" Rose asked.

"No."

Rose tried to decipher Lori's words.

"Brian, you'd better go upstairs and see what Lori's talking about. Check and see if Dawn got into Kathy's razors. I'll stay with Lori and the baby."

Brian raced up the stairs. He stared into Dawn's bedroom. The child lay on the floor, covered in blood. He backed out toward the bathroom, turned and spotted Kathy's nude body on the floor, bathed in a sea of congealed red gore. Both appeared dead.

Brian dashed down the stairs to face Rose. "Kathy's on the bathroom floor. Dawn is in the bedroom. Blood is everywhere. Both look dead. Should I call the police?"

Rose gasped, barely able to mouth her words. "Yes, do it now."

Brian picked up the phone and dialed.

Rose handed the baby to Lori and scurried to a neighboring house. She pounded on the door for what seemed an eternity until a teenage girl appeared.

"Why didn't you answer the door?"

"I didn't hear you," replied the girl. "What's wrong?"

"Something happened at Kathy's. I am not sure what, but you have to call an ambulance."

Lori followed her mother, carrying baby Dino in her arms. The neighbor girl's sister appeared at the door and took the infant from Lori. Barging into the house, Lori phoned for an ambulance. She next called V&R Industries, demanding to speak with Lou Kadunce. The secretary informed her that Lou had left for lunch.

"Have him call home as soon as he returns. This is an emergency."

A few minutes later, Lori redialed V&R. "Is Lou back yet? He's not! Listen, have him go home immediately as soon as he returns. There's a real bad situation at his house."

Still shaking, Lori stifled a sniffle. Rose, her eyes brimming with tears, reached out and stroked her daughter's hair. That was all she could do.

Dispatcher Lastoria at the New Castle Police Department took Brian Baer's call and gathered the pertinent facts.

"Easy son, slow down. Now, give me your name and spell it. Uh huh, Brian Baer. That's B-A-E-R. Okay." Lastoria jotted down the name and address. "Yes, 702 Wilmington Avenue. You say there are two bodies. Now listen, stay calm, do not touch anything, leave the house and do not go back. Wait outside for a patrol car. It should be there within ten minutes. We are only a few blocks away." Lastoria paused to listen to the voice at the other end of the line. "Yes, stay at the back of the house. Someone will be there right away."

Lastoria hung up the phone and dropped his pen. He paused a beat before turning to a fellow officer. "McGuirk, head up to 702 Wilmington on the double. I think we have a double homicide on our hands."

2

THE CRIME SCENE

Turn-officer Arthur McGuirk and his associate Robert Keys streaked to the Kadunce house in a squad car with the siren screaming. After questioning Baer, the police proceeded through the back door and upstairs to investigate. As soon as McGuirk checked out the two dead bodies, he called Detective Lieutenant Leon Sasiadek and the coroner's office.

Sasiadek notified Detective-Sergeant George Kennedy, a jovial twenty-eight-year veteran nicknamed "Jake" by his pals.

"Jake, return to base at once," the radio barked.

"Roger, on my way."

At the station, Jake met up with his lieutenant. Officer Ron Williams usually handled photography at crime scenes, but he was off duty. No big deal. Jake and Sas could handle the camera. Kennedy liked working with the lieutenant, a man who kept to himself, but a darn smart cop who knew his job.

Kennedy and Sasiadek reached the Kadunce house shortly after two o'clock in the afternoon. McGuirk and Keys had already secured the building.

"It's bad up there, real bad," Keys offered.

Kennedy eased up the stairs, keeping his eyes open for anything out of place. In the bathroom, his eyes fixed on the female corpse spread across the floor. He gagged at the bloody stench of death beneath him. Victim Kathleen Buckel Kadunce lay facedown, slathered in blood, her head resting near the corner of the tub, her hands tucked beneath her body, her left foot resting beside the toilet. She was nude except for a pair of purple socks on her feet and a Timex watch with a black leatherette strap on her wrist. A bullet had cut through the left side of her skull. Seventeen knife wounds sliced through Mrs. Kadunce's back and neck, as if she had been cut in some ghoulish ritual. Red splatter stained the blue ceramic tile walls. A .22-caliber slug rested in the corner on the floor in a puddle of congealed blood. A pair of glasses sat atop the vanity. Someone had tossed a cigarette butt at the base of the tub and a second by the victim's head. An ashtray, a Marvel comic book and a roll of toilet paper sat above the commode tank.

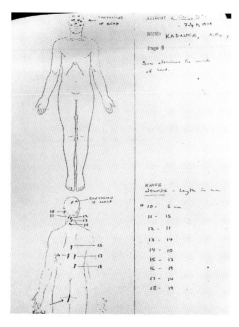

Wound diagram, Kathy Kadunce. *Courtesy of the New Castle Police Department.*

Death had cast an aura of innocence on the twenty-five-year-old mother. With the color drained from her ashen face, Kathy's skin appeared soft, smooth and unblemished. At five feet, nine inches and 145 pounds, her body retained some of the chunkiness from her recent pregnancy. The combination of youth and death compounded the atrocity of the crime.

A lack of defensive wounds suggested that Kathy's attackers had butchered her like a sacrificial lamb, quickly and savagely. No evidence of sexual assault was apparent, a fact the autopsy would later confirm.

"Poor kid," Kennedy said. He had witnessed death before but never grew used to it. His heartbeat quickened to a staccato beat. The day's lunch rumbled in his gut. Death often strikes swiftly and without warning. As he pieced together the viciousness of the slaughter, his eyes searched for leads, a motive, anything to bring sense to the crime.

If the mother's murder gnawed at Kennedy, the killing across the hall tore into his innards. Four-year-old Dawn Kadunce lay on her left side on the bedroom floor, her hands outstretched as if begging God for mercy, her body sliced open like a dissected laboratory rat. Blood from seventeen

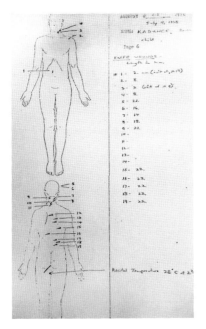

Wound diagram, Dawn Kadunce.
Courtesy of the New Castle Police Department.

knife wounds soaked through her yellow-footed nightie decorated with pink and green animals. Red splotches covered the north and east walls, staining the floral sheets on her bed and the blue shag rug on the floor.

"What butcher would do this?" Kennedy asked. "Almost three decades on the force and now this." Like lightning gathering force during a spring storm, the acid in Kennedy's innards gathered steam and attacked again. He sucked in a deep breath of air to calm his emotions. He was a cop and had work to do.

As the sergeant scoured the house for crime debris, Anthony DeCarbo of DeCarbo Ambulance ushered Howard Reynolds, the county coroner, upstairs to the crime scene. Reynolds, a funeral director and father of four, relished peace and quiet. He spent hours carving award-winning duck decoys at home or fishing in Neshannock Creek. The gruesome sight of the dead four-year-old sickened him. After a few perfunctory questions to Kennedy, the coroner checked his watch. 2:38 p.m. Like Kennedy, he inhaled, exhaled slowly and mustered up his strength. He cut a slit through Dawn's nightie to check the child's body temperature with a rectal thermometer in order to ascertain the approximate time of death. A reading of twenty-eight degrees Celsius indicated a time of death between six and nine o'clock in the morning. After additional examinations of the victims, Reynolds phoned Dr. William Gillespie to arrange a double autopsy.

While police probed the downstairs seeking evidence, Kennedy drew a chalk outline around the body of the child to mark the crime scene. Minutes later, he followed the same grim procedure for the mother.

When Sasiadek left the room to retrieve his camera, Kennedy walked downstairs and out the back door for a cigarette to calm his nerves. The smoke break didn't help. The vision of the butchered child rocked his brain. He returned upstairs with Sasiadek to photograph the bodies. Each snap of the shutter reinforced the brutality of the killings. Silently, he mouthed

Right: The bathroom crime scene at the Kadunce house. *Courtesy of the New Castle Police Department.*

Below: Dawn Kadunce's body. *Courtesy of the New Castle Police Department.*

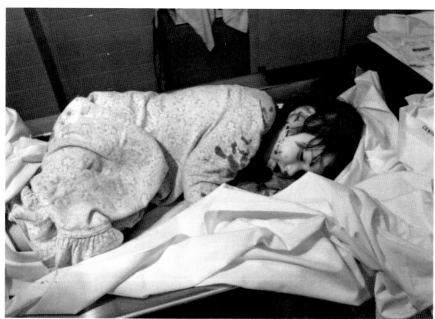

a prayer for the little girl's soul. Kennedy knew he would sleep fitfully that night, if at all.

The innocence of Dawn's stuffed panda propped on the dresser, the Raggedy Ann doll lying on a nearby table and the hodgepodge of toys scattered across the floor contrasted vividly with the horror of the child's bloody body sprawled across a green blanket on the bedroom floor.

Kennedy catalogued the site quickly but accurately. He drew a rough sketch of the rooms and jotted down salient particulars on his notepad. No detail can be too small in a murder investigation. He listed Dawn's toys on the floor: her toy refrigerator, a stuffed dog, a *Sesame Street* house, a doll coloring book and a pair of Mickey Mouse sandals. He even noted the multicolored curtains while trying to avoid the tiny body below him.

Nosy nellies, spotting the activity around the house, began to pry. Officer Keys guarded the front door and Klingensmith the back to protect the crime scene from contamination. Meanwhile, Captain William Carbone, a square-shouldered dapper martinet with a helmet-like toupee and a cocksure swagger, appeared to relieve Lieutenant McGuirk and take charge of the case. After inspecting Dawn's bedroom and the bathroom, he directed a cursory search of the first floor. The house appeared normal other than the upstairs carnage.

"I've never seen a worse one. Get hold of Gagliardo, and let's get this investigation in full swing," Carbone ordered a subordinate. The captain concealed his frayed nerves by barking out commands to control the fact-finding.

Despite Sergeant Frank Gagliardo's assignment to juvenile, Carbone respected his skill as a homicide detective. Mayor Francis Rogan had appointed Gagliardo as the police captain in 1972. During Rogan's second term, he promoted Carbone to captain. Although Gagliardo's Italian temper made him quick to anger, he forged a survivor's mentality and accepted the demotion to sergeant as part of New Castle's political system. "Gig," as his friends on the force called him, was an action junkie who adapted to the reduced rank in juvenile and caused no waves.

Larrry Kadunce, "Lou" as everyone called him, returned from lunch at Murphy's in the Towne Mall shortly after 2:00 p.m. Ron Silvis, his nephew and coworker, accompanied him in the car back to V&R, where the plant manager met them at the parking lot.

"Someone called you, Lou. You'd better get home at once."

"What's the matter?"

"Don't know, some kind of accident. You'd better head home right away."

Silvis hopped out of the car to return to work, and Lou raced home. Parking his light-blue Buick in the Jefferson Street driveway at the rear of the house, Lou stepped out of his car. A policeman was guarding the back door.

"Who are you?" queried the cop.

"I'm Lou Kadunce. I live here. What's going on?"

"Go ahead in."

Opening the storm door, Kadunce entered the empty kitchen. He heard voices from the next room. Glancing toward the dining room, he spotted Brian Baer speaking to a uniformed cop. Off to the side, Carbone, dressed in street clothes, spoke to another policeman. Balding, midsize Gagliardo, wearing a T-shirt and jeans, stood in the corner like a mannequin, a scowl etched into his face. He had been off duty but sped to the Kadunce house as soon as he received a call without bothering to change.

"What's going on here?" a confused Kadunce asked.

"Are you Lou Kadunce?" replied Captain Carbone.

"Yes," Kadunce answered.

"Mr. Baer, that's all for now." A uniform escorted him from the room. "Mr. Kadunce, please sit down. I'm afraid I have some bad news." Carbone paused. "Your wife is dead."

"What?...Where is she?"

"Upstairs."

Kadunce rose from his seat. "Can I see her?"

"Better not. You see, she's been murdered, and it's not a pretty sight."

Lou spoke in a monotone. "I can take it. I was in Vietnam." He stared at the officer blankly, awaiting an answer.

"Sorry, Mr. Kadunce. Please sit. We can't allow you to go upstairs. Your daughter is there, too." Carbone noted a stoic lack of emotion from the husband.

"Where's my son?"

"He's fine and is next door."

"What happened?"

"We're not sure yet. Do you have any idea?"

Kadunce shook his head.

"Listen, does anything down here look out of the ordinary?" Carbone asked, seeking clues.

Kadunce rose and scanned the room, glancing from side to side. Scratching his head, he pointed to an ashtray. "That usually isn't there. Hey, where is Dawn's doll?"

"Is this it?" answered a policeman, pointing to a doll behind the door.

"Yea, that's it." Kadunce continued his search. He noticed a frying pan on the stove containing uncooked potatoes and a half-empty cup of coffee on the dining room table. "That wasn't there when I left for work." He pointed to the dirty dishes in the sink. "I don't remember those when I left this morning, and Kathy rarely drank coffee." Kadunce mentioned nothing else.

Gagliardo silently watched Kadunce. Standard police investigative procedure demanded a rigorous examination of a surviving spouse in the absence of a clear-cut suspect. While Carbone relayed detail after detail of the brutal killings, the husband displayed minimal reaction to the tragedy—no tears, no curses, no threats. Gagliardo bristled. His volcanic temper would spew lava at the slightest hint of harm to his own family. He had difficulty accepting this man's dispassionate response to his wife and daughter's deaths. Lou Kadunce sat like a knot on a log, wordlessly, as if in a trance. Could he be in shock? Maybe, but Gig would have questioned Saint Francis of Assisi had he responded with such apathy.

Gagliardo exited the room. Carrying a cup of steaming coffee from the kitchen in his right hand, he drifted upstairs to see if Jake needed help.

"You look terrible," Gig commented.

"I can't understand this kind of thing, Gig."

"Nor can I, Jake. We'll get the bastards who did this. Mark my words, we'll get them."

"Here." Gig handed the coffee to Jake. "This will calm you down. I'll be back later."

"Hey, Gig."

"Yeah, Jake?"

"Thanks."

Gig returned to the dining room to watch and listen. He observed Kadunce sitting quietly on a chair, his elbows resting on the table, his head in his hands, unshaken, as if bothered by some minor bump in the road rather than this violent loss. Gig wondered what made him tick—might be shock, but maybe not. He pulled Carbone aside.

"Captain, something don't seem right. Kadunce acts like a zombie. You and me would be climbing the walls if we were in his shoes. He's too cool. Let's give this guy a paraffin test. He may have gunpowder on his hands. After the test we can haul his butt down to the station for questioning."

Carbone agreed. He shared Gig's suspicions. Besides, he had uncovered an inconsistency in Kadunce's story. When asked the last time he had spoken to his wife, the husband hesitated. He said he thought she had been asleep when he left at 7:00 a.m. Later, he changed his story. He remembered Kathy sitting up in bed and feeding Dino. He even recalled telling his wife goodbye when he left.

"We haven't found evidence of forced entry," interrupted a uniformed cop. "And no sign of a struggle between the deceased and her assailants."

"Thanks," Carbone answered, fairly certain Kathy knew her killer, or killers.

The telephone rang. A cop answered. "Sergeant McGuirk speaking. Yes, ma'am, Mr. Kadunce is here." McGuirk turned to Lou and handed Kadunce the phone. "It's for you. It's your mother-in-law."

"Yes, it's true. Kathy and Dawn are dead. I don't think you'd better come over yet. I have to go." Kadunce handed the phone back to McGuirk, who hung up the receiver.

As the clock moved toward 3:30 p.m., Carbone ordered Lieutenant Malley, a recent arrival, to search the perimeter of the property for evidence. He sent Officer Klingensmith to check the roof of the Fast 'n Friendly store next door. The hunt proved fruitless.

Unaware of the investigation underway, thirty-six-year-old policeman Chuck Abraham purchased a card for his wife at Towne Mall in downtown New Castle. It was his wife's birthday and also a day off for him. Those who knew Chuck considered him a plodder. As a seven-year-old, he delivered newspapers to earn spending money. During his preteens, he matched suit pants and coats for a neighbor who owned a laundry. In high school, he bagged groceries at the A&M Supermarket after school. This up-and-comer, known as "Babe" to his friends, had been promoted from narcotics in '75, after only seven years on the force.

As he drove up Wilmington, flashing lights from the bevy of cruisers and yellow crime-scene tape drew him like a moth to the flame. He slowed the car. A patrolman in blues puffed on a cigarette outside the Kadunce house, his eyes darting back and forth. Everything seemed under control, probably just a drug bust. Abraham put his foot to the gas and headed home. He could check out the action at the station the next morning.

"Inventory everything. Check the doors and windows again to be sure they haven't been tampered with. Look for anything to help us sort out this mess," Carbone hollered. While the cops scoured through the kitchen and living room seeking clues, Carbone returned to his questioning.

"Am I a suspect?" Kadunce asked.

Carbone readjusted a button on his shirt and stared Kadunce in the eye. "Yes, I'm afraid so. Do you want to call someone?"

"Yes, I'd like to call an attorney." Kadunce immediately thought of Lou Pomerico, his law teacher at New Castle Business College, where he took night classes.

"Better read him his rights," Carbone ordered. While Kadunce and Carbone arranged for legal representation with the district attorney's office, Bo DeCarbo and an assistant packed the blood-soaked corpses in individual green vinyl bags and hauled them by ambulance to the St. Francis Hospital morgue for an autopsy. County coroner Howard Reynolds followed in his own car.

Attorney Lou Pomerico received a call from Assistant District Attorney Howard Klebe around 3:45 p.m. After absorbing a few details of the case, Pomerico proceeded to the house. A crowd had gathered outside to gawk and gossip. Kathy's father and brother lingered among the onlookers, anxiously seeking details. Pulsating red and white lights from the police cruisers heightened the pressure on the young attorney facing his first big case, and the mass of humanity parted for him like the Red Sea for Moses.

Pomerico heard a whisper: "That guy's a lawyer. There's only one reason he's here. Lou must be involved. Where there's smoke, there's usually fire."

Ignoring the gawkers, Pomerico marched up the stairs, and a uniformed policeman ushered him into the dining room. The attorney saw Lou Kadunce, a student in his business law class at New Castle Business College, sitting at a table. He remembered him as an introvert who rarely took part in open discussions.

After shaking hands and offering his condolences, Pomerico took his client to the back of the kitchen to discuss the case in private. Lou dragged on a cigarette, pacing the floor. He exhaled a burst of smoke. His hands were shaking, and he stared at the wall. Kadunce's red eyes and general demeanor convinced Pomerico that his client was shaken and suffering from shock. Kadunce eventually spoke: "I can't believe this happened. Who would do this?"

"Lou, you've got to keep your composure. We have to go over the facts."

Carbone watched the conference between attorney and client for several minutes before approaching. "We'll need a formal statement from Mr. Kadunce. Can we proceed to the station now?"

"He's been through a lot this afternoon. Let's give him a break. We'll come to the station tomorrow."

"Yea, I guess you're right, but first I'd like him to take a paraffin test."

"Just a minute!" Pomerico huddled with his client to explain how a neuron activation-analysis test worked. "Lou, I'm not saying you did anything, but if you don't want to take the test you don't have to."

"No, I want to cooperate. I have nothing to hide."

"Okay, he'll take the test."

A state trooper swabbed a 5 percent nitric acid solution on Kadunce's hands to check for residual gunpowder stains. The test proved negative. Kadunce also consented to a search of his car, which turned up nothing of interest. Kadunce and Pomerico agreed to meet Carbone and the investigating team at the station the following morning at eleven o'clock.

Around four o'clock, Reverend Clarence Drake of the Evangel Community Church, the minister who married Kathy and Lou in 1972, appeared on the front porch. After explaining who he was, the minister entered the house escorted by an uniformed officer. Kathy's family had alerted him to the deaths of two of his parishioners. As Lou sat at a table surrounded by detectives, Reverend Drake offered soothing words. When Drake paused, Carbone took him aside.

"We're finished with Mr. Kadunce for today, but he can't stay here tonight. We've got to seal off the house and protect the crime scene. I'm sure you understand. Would you help him get some of his clothing?" Carbone asked.

Reverend Drake took Kadunce's arm, and the two men walked upstairs to retrieve a few articles of clothing. A policeman accompanied them into the bedroom. To ensure the integrity of the evidence, he watched while Kadunce packed.

When Kadunce returned downstairs, Carbone met him. "You're free to go, Mr. Kadunce. See you tomorrow at eleven. Okay?"

Kadunce nodded his head in agreement.

Lou carried his clothing onto the porch. He barely acknowledged Kathy's family. A friend, Bill Howley, emerged to drive him to his mother's, where family and friends gathered to comfort him. Lou had fourteen brothers and sisters—people sat and stood everywhere, some offering sympathy, others asking questions.

As the evening wore on, the impact of the day's tragedy took full effect. Lou's distress intensified, and he had difficulty standing still. His infant child had been taken to his brother Harry and his wife Carol's house. The need to be with his son drew him like iron to a magnet. He needed to hold his child and sort out his thoughts.

Lou slipped out of his mother's house and drove to Harry and Carol's, where he spent the night. Dino was sleeping on the couch. Lou parked himself on the floor beneath the baby, his hands cradling his son's tiny fingers. Eventually, he fell asleep, ending the worst day in his life.

3

THE GAGLIARDOS

Sergeant Frank Gagliardo departed the Kadunce house shortly after 6:00 p.m. for his Vine Street home. He was bushed. As Gig opened the door, his wife, Shelvie, was putting the finishing touches on dinner in the kitchen.

"Are the boys home?" Gig asked, referring to eighteen-year-old Joe and fourteen-year-old Sam.

"They're upstairs. You look dog tired. Rough day?"

"Yeah." Frank sighed, telling his wife about the double murders and the ensuing investigation. Shelvie listened in silence.

"You know what I think?"

"What?" answered Frank, keenly aware of his wife's ability to ferret out simple solutions to complex problems.

"I think the husband was involved. Remember the Merryman-Reno killing a while back?"

"Yeah." Gig recalled the earlier robbery-murder case.

"I told you the guy with blood on his tennis shoes that your pal Chuck Abraham picked up after a fender bender had done the killing."

"Sure, I remember."

"I said the guy was too dumb to change his shoes," Shelvie continued.

Gig laughed. Chuck couldn't believe a killer wouldn't wipe the blood off his shoes after committing murder. The guy was really dumb, and Shelvie had picked up on it.

Lieutenant Frank Gagliardo. *Courtesy of the New Castle Police Department.*

"Yeah, and you were right."

"Maybe I'm right again."

"Maybe," he answered, thinking that Shelvie might just make a darn good detective.

4

THE INTERROGATION

Lou Kadunce and Attorney Pomerico entered the bowels of the police station to continue the previous day's questioning.

"Mr. Kadunce, let's get started. Take a seat please." Captain Carbone opened. "Okay, tell us where you were the night before the murders."

The husband recalled coming home after work on Monday and showering. He left home around five o'clock for the classes he took at New Castle Business College under the VA program. He grabbed a bite in the cafeteria before attending Lou Pomerico's six o'clock business law class. After a short break, he attended a psychology class where he engaged instructor Barbara Klenotic in a lively discussion on male household power. Usually quiet, Lou argued that a "wife had no right to criticize her husband about his friends and job." Lou wanted answers, but he received none. To keep the class on target, the teacher changed the subject. Kadunce left class early to cash his veteran's check at the Giant Eagle Supermarket.

"I returned home to watch *20/20* on television before going to bed."

The day of the murders, Kadunce awoke at 6:30 a.m. He thought he dressed for work in shorts and a pullover shirt, but he couldn't be certain. Although his recollection was fuzzy, he felt fairly certain he said goodbye to Dino and Kathy. Dawn remained asleep in her bedroom.

"Wait a minute." Carbone interrupted "I thought Kathy was still asleep when you left for work. That's what you said yesterday."

"No, I think I said goodbye to her. She was feeding Dino."

New Castle Police Department Office in the city building. *Author's collection.*

"I see." Carbone paused for effect as he took in the discrepancy. "What did you do next?"

"I drove to work." At first, Kadunce recalled driving downtown on Wilmington Road, turning left on Washington at the square.

Carbone knew the questioning game well. "I thought the square was blocked?" Redevelopment Authority construction had blocked that turn to traffic, another discrepancy.

"Oh yeah, you're right." Kadunce rethought his route. He traveled down Highland instead of Wilmington. "After picking up my nephew Ron Silvis, I stopped at Lawson's for a Pepsi and a pack of cigarettes. Then I bought a couple dollars of gas at the Big Bear."

During the questioning, Kadunce talked about his marriage. "Kathy and I had problems like all young people, mostly concerning money, but problems don't make you stop loving your family." Lou described how he dropped out of high school in the twelfth grade for a job at American Cyanamide. After a month, he enlisted in the air force and was stationed at Lackland, Texas. He specialized in security, gaining proficiency with the M-16 rifle and the

New Castle City Square. *Author's collection.*

.38-caliber pistol. He served most of 1970 and 1971 in Vietnam, where he accidentally shot himself in the foot.

After discharge, he met Kathy, who worked at Orange Julius in the Towne Mall. He caught odd jobs at the Fassinger Company and Consolidated Pipe and later worked as an assistant manager at a gas station and as a laborer with a construction company prior to landing his current spot as a foreman with V&R, a sink manufacturer on Grove Street.

Kathy and Lou married in 1972. The couple were living on Crawford Avenue when Dawn was born on May 15, 1974. They moved to Wilmington Avenue before Robert's birth on May 9, 1978. Both Kathy and Lou liked sports, especially football. She rooted for the Kansas City Chiefs; he was a fan of the Pittsburgh Steelers. Lou sometimes called Kathy "Skid" and Dawn "Lizzy" or "Pumpkin." Lou's eyes glazed over when he mentioned the nicknames to the police.

Wrapping up, Carbone pondered the morning's questioning. Kadunce had changed his route to work from his earlier statement, but his nephew Ron Silvis later confirmed the second itinerary. Silvis also stated under oath that he had made a pass at Kathy and Lou may have had some brief fling with a girl at work named Mary Akers.

Kadunce served time in the Lawrence County Jail in 1973 for four separate incidents of indecent exposure after neighbor Carolyn Anastasia reported him for walking nude in his backyard. Mrs. Anastasia had caught him again taking out the garbage in the nude on the Monday morning preceding the murders. The Anastasias intended to confront Lou, but the murder occurred before they could do so.

Even without a proven motive and only minimal evidence, Carbone's police instinct honed in on Lou Kadunce as his primary suspect. He ordered officer David Kelty to tail him, but the surveillance yielded nothing. Photos taken at the funeral provided no leads. Gagliardo razzed Attorney Pomerico about his "pervert client" to irritate him. Officers James Carungi and Richard Smith logged seventy-eight hours of overtime questioning neighbors to no avail.

The police continued to hound Lou Kadunce, hoping he would snap, but the husband stuck to his story. Without a weapon, a solid motive or any real clues, the investigation stalled.

The September 15, 1978 *New Castle News* headline reported: "Police Stymied in Their Investigation." Carbone reacted with a terse quote: "We're not sleeping on it. We've been working."

Lou Kadunce continued to work at V&R and attend New Castle Business College in the evenings. He told the newspaper: "I'm just trying to live day by day. I don't even want to think about it." Lou moved from the Wilmington Street home to his brother's house, where he and Dino stayed. The Anastasias remodeled and rented out the former Kadunce house.

Lou Kadunce booking photo. *Courtesy of the New Castle Police Department.*

Kathy's father, Richard Buckel, offered a $5,000 reward for information leading to the conviction of the killer or killers. He told the newspaper in November 1979: "Had my daughter and granddaughter been killed in an auto accident, I could accept it. I hope to God the killer turns himself in so that he can be helped and won't do it again. I can't believe that God wanted those kids to go that way."

The police continued the hunt through 1979. Carbone likened the case to the unsolved and seemingly motiveless killings of four-year-old Melanie Gargasz and her thirty-seven-year-old babysitter Beverly Withers on November 6, 1975. When Melanie's mother returned from work around 4:00 p.m., she discovered her daughter and the babysitter on a bed, murdered by multiple bullets fired from a small-caliber firearm. Mrs. Withers was nude, but the autopsy revealed no sign of sexual assault.

After months of fruitless inquiry, police efforts on the Kadunce murders declined. Other crimes cried out for immediate attention. By January 1980, the Dawn and Kathy Kadunce killings, like the earlier Gargasz-Withers case, had been relegated to the unsolved murder files.

5

COSTAL

R un, run, as fast as you can! Here comes Frank the devil man!" chanted the neighborhood kids playing kick the can as the strange man with the long beard lumbered down the sidewalk outside hearing range. His piercing green eyes and scraggly hair scared even the bravest. Long before the game ended, the youngest had raced home before the onset of darkness to outrun fears of the night and the devil man, Frank Costal.

On Monday, January 22, 1979, fifty-one-year-old Costal awakened shortly after noon. The day before, the Pittsburgh Steelers locked up Super Bowl XIII with a 35–31 win over the Cowboys. Terry Bradshaw earned the most valuable player award, but Frank couldn't care less. He was not a sports fan. Greeting the early afternoon with a guttural grunt, he yanked the blanket across his ballooning stomach and hairy chest using his right hand. With his left, he wiped the shoulder-length hair from his eyes. The dreary Pennsylvania winter drew a shiver from his body. He scratched his upper arm, where "Gypsy" had been tattooed next to the names "Tex, Dan and Lee," reminders of his carnival past. "Gypsy" reminded him of the bright costumes, the pageantry and the harlequin characters that made carnival life strange and exciting.

Remaining in bed, Costal imagined a magic carpet lifting him across time to the carnival midway and the sweet aroma of onions, peppers and grease-soaked sausages frying on the grill. Bevies of lanky ladies with caked-on makeup, skimpy tops and tight polyester slacks ambled past him. The shrill

Frank Costal and friend.
Courtesy of the New Castle
Police Department.

din of children begging their parents for cotton candy and candy apples rippled through his head.

As the carnival backlot took shape in his mind, Costal could hear the spiel of the barker in his flame-red jacket hawking the sideshow:

> *Ladies and gents, step right up, see the remarkable alligator boy. He walks. He talks. He slithers like a reptile. Watch ostrich man regurgitate a golf ball and a live mouse right before your eyes. Yes, folks, you heard me, a live mouse. We have damsels and dwarfs, the human torch, the bearded lady, the tattooed man, the fire eater and the sword swallower, all manner of freaks and geeks, guaranteed to amaze your sensibilities. See the creature of the night, the giant cat with fang-like teeth. Watch him gnarl and gnash. And we have Frankie-Francine—is he a man or a woman? You can judge for yourselves. Come right in—only twenty-five cents. Don't dare miss it.*

Gypsy, like the gypsy in stripper Gypsy Rose Lee, like a band of gypsies roaming from town to town living off the fat of the land, like the gypsy fortune-tellers who knew the future, Frank Costal was a gypsy, anxious to inhale all life offered.

Frank Costal was born in Cleveland Heights, Ohio, on February 28, 1928. His father, a rough-hewn Hungarian immigrant, worked as a mechanic. His Romanian-born mother drudged as a hospital housekeeper.

While young Frank was in grade school, the family moved to New Castle, where his father caught a job as a maintenance man with the Royal Cafe and as a trailer park supervisor.

Frank frequently clashed with his father, a strict disciplinarian with a hot temper and an eye for the ladies. His son's unusual ways irritated and revolted him. "You're no son of mine. You don't deserve to be called Kostal"—the original spelling of the Costal name. The senior Kostal's old-world toughness and physical abuse alienated Frank, who danced to his own music. When his father beat him, as he often did, Frank simmered with hate. After his old man mistreated his mother, Costal plotted revenge. When life at home grew intolerable, the fourteen-year-old quit school, jumped on a flatbed railway car and skipped out of town to join the carnival. The authorities collected him in Sumter, South Carolina, and forced him to return home. The New Castle police soon arrested Frank for stealing a bicycle but released him because of his age and clean record. To avoid his father, he ran away from home a second time to rejoin the carnival, changing the spelling of his name from Kostal to Costal.

The carnival served as Frank's finishing school, teaching him how to survive, accepting and nurturing his homosexuality, providing him with sanctuary and acting as his surrogate father. Barkers and hawkers, acrobats and clowns, double-dealers and pickpockets became his Harvard and Yale professors. He picked up fortunetelling from an old black woman from the Florida Everglades. Combining clues from the lines on the mark's palm along with hints derived from clothing styles, speech patterns, age, physical size, astrological sign and sex, Costal would present a picture of future events. Carny pals encouraged Frank to dig into Satanism and black magic. The deeper he looked, the stronger the pull of the occult grew.

Frank performed a variety of jobs with the carnival. Clad in a crimson jacket with gold buttons, he twirled a rope for an aerial ballet artist to music. He loved to dress in costume. He became a drag queen in Louisville with the Amusements of America Corporation, calling himself "Frankie-Francine," the hermaphroditic half-man, half-woman—an extraordinary and wonderful role for him. He worked the midway games with Ringling Brothers, set up a rodeo at Soldier's Field in Chicago and toured half the country by rail with the Johnny Jones Exposition as a roustabout.

Costal assembled bleachers and drove spikes to support tents. When finished, he might change into a uniform and usher spectators to seats in the reserved section under the big top. He even sewed costumes and assisted the noted wig producer Clio Rennet.

Police photo of teenage Frank Costal after stealing a bicycle. *Courtesy of the New Castle Police Department.*

While traveling the southern route, he took in a chain gang laboring beneath the Georgia sun under the watchful eyes of armed guards. He relished his own freedom to come and go as he wished. To the north, he gaped at the Indians whooping it up in Sabrina, Ontario. Like a will-o'-the-wisp, Costal moved from one company to the next, one job to the next, depending on the season, the money and his own appetite for excitement.

Costal evolved like a caterpillar emerging from its cocoon into a fully developed butterfly, unique and spiritually attuned to the auras flying around him. Frank changed his appearance. He grew a long mane of hair. The boyish freshness disappeared from his face. He drank in the carny mantra, viewing the mass of humanity as prey—suckers designed for easy picking. Life on the midway involved a series of rackets. The crafty man worked these rackets to his advantage. No one really won at carnival games. Pay a quarter to knock down the pins, and you might win a prize worth half that amount. Frank learned these lessons well.

Toward the tail end of World War II, caught up by a combination of patriotism and the draw of the uniform, the sixteen-year-old lied about his age and left the carnival to enlist in the military. He envisioned medals and parades. Instead, he received discipline, regimentation, orders and rules—the very reasons he had run away from his father. Like the Georgia chain gangs, he felt trapped by the military. In August 1946, Costal received a reprimand for petty larceny, later serving time in the stockade for going AWOL.

Following his discharge, Costal, like the gypsy he was, moved from one mill job to the next. During the Korean War, he grew bored with civilian life and reenlisted as Frank Batzel, a last name he snitched from his stepfather. He served as a patrolman along the East German border but suffered a nervous breakdown and received an honorable discharge on March 5, 1956.

Frank Costal military photo (standing to reader's right). *Courtesy of the New Castle Police Department.*

Costal drifted through a variety of jobs: spray painter at Pittsburgh Forge and Dodge Cork, laborer with White Owl Cigar and crane man at American Bridge. He had become openly gay. In the mill town of Aliquippa, he walked into a biker's bar, nicknamed the "Punch and Drink Club," wearing a jean jacket with the name "Dragons" sewn across the back.

"Who the hell are the Dragons?" asked a biker known as "Fighting Phil."

"It's Drag-ons, not Dragons," Costal giggled.

Fighting Phil failed to see the humor. He picked up his beer bottle and smashed it on Costal's head. Blood splashed from the wound, which required several stitches at the local hospital.

Spinal bone chips from an industrial injury at American Bridge qualified Costal for disability payments. During the 1970s, he lived on a government check of $240 per month. He earned a few dollars under the radar by doing maintenance jobs around his Highland Avenue apartment building in New Castle and from the sale of string art.

Costal had lots of free time. He spent much of it with the teenagers in and around the projects, who looked up to this odd man with a hypnotic personality. He gravitated to the boys with peach-fuzz faces and thin physiques. In 1977, he had an affair with Paul Werblinger, a special needs high school dropout and ex-con in his late twenties. When Costal discovered Werblinger playing cards and flirting with a woman across the hall, he chased his former lover out of the building with a sword. The two made up but split permanently after Werblinger and Jim Antoniotti received two-and-a-half-year sentences at Western Penitentiary for robbing Pete's Bait Shop.

Costal orchestrated a mock wedding with nineteen-year-old high school dropout Marshall Dillon in 1979. Three teenage boys—Steve Hammond, James Zingaro and Randy Perrotta—witnessed the ceremony and signed the certificate Costal designed. The boys assumed it all to be one big joke. Frank considered the marriage a serious affair. When the bisexual Dillon confessed his preference for women, Costal chased him with the same sword he used to threaten Werblinger. Dillon fled the apartment without bothering to pick up his personal belongings.

Frank felt a special attraction to slow-witted Mike Atkinson, a hulking troublemaker who preferred women to men but accepted Costal's advances on occasion.

Costal sat up in bed, opened his mouth and yawned, exposing his lack of teeth, a reminder of a motorcycle accident that might just as easily have killed him. His breath stank like Limburger cheese from the Black Label beers he had chugged while watching television the prior night. He opened

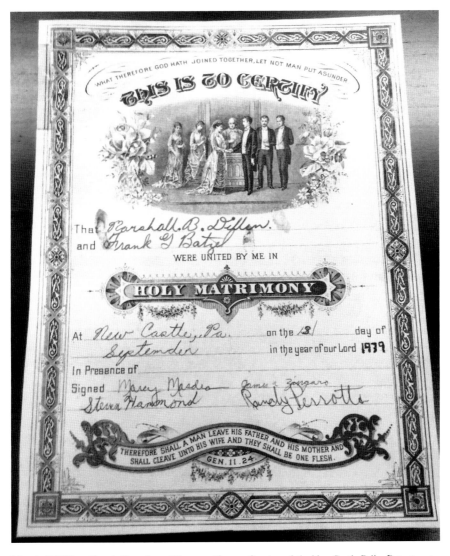

Marshall Dillon–Frank Costal wedding certificate. *Courtesy of the New Castle Police Department.*

the book *Man, Myth and Magic* to page 22 and quickly closed it—didn't feel like reading. His bladder ached. Once he relieved himself, he returned to his bed and jotted a few notes in his diary. Checking his horoscope, he read: "Personal relationships should show considerable improvement." Costal grinned and put the blue *Fingerhut Daily Horoscope* back on the table by his bed.

At nearly 1:00 p.m., Costal donned a green flannel shirt and dark baggy pants. He added a coat, lumbered out of his apartment and headed down the Highland Avenue hill. Reaching into his pocket, he snagged his last Pall Mall. Crumbling the pack and flipping it on the sidewalk, he lit up and sucked the smoke into his lungs. As the wind blew through his shoulder-length hair and long gray-flecked beard, he exhaled through his thick lips.

Blue heart-shaped tattoos, courtesy of Sailor Bill from Wheeling, West Virginia, marked each of Costal's earlobes. A skull and crossbones earring dangled from his right ear. Around his neck, he sported a circular pentagram disk with the face of Satan protruding from its center, an anathema to the predominantly Catholic community in which he lived.

Deep furrows indented Costal's forehead. Scars from a motorcycle accident etched his face, and thin blue veins lined his bulbous nose. His eyelids sagged. A broken eardrum, probably caused from a childhood beating, hampered his hearing. Pockmarked cheeks amplified his ominous appearance. Massive in size, nearly six feet tall and well over two hundred pounds, he resembled Grigori Rasputin, the Siberian mystic who mesmerized the family of Czar Nicholas II of Russia during the early twentieth century.

Frank Costal. *Courtesy of the New Castle Police Department.*

An older couple walking in the opposite direction near the Scottish Rite Cathedral cleared a wide berth to allow Costal to pass. Strangers avoided the "Witch of Highland Avenue." The woman whispered in her husband's ear. The man nodded in agreement and put his finger to his lips to hush his wife's recognition. Costal liked when people feared him.

Proceeding down the hill onto Washington Street, New Castle's main drag, Costal glanced into the Perelman's Jewelry window to admire the flashing psychedelic lights surrounding an Electrophonic stereo. Continuing his trek, he halted at the Diamond to take in the statue of the unknown Civil War soldier in the center of the square. He turned left at the alley leading to the Central Barber Shop. Its sign read, "We need your head to run our business." Inside, Mike Carvella was cutting hair.

Central Barber Shop. *Courtesy of Michele Perelman and the Lawrence County Historical Society*

Costal popped his head through the door. "Hi, Mike." Frank liked the barber, who once loaned him a few bucks.

His brother Pete, whom everyone called "Figo," stepped out of the back room.

"How you doing, Frankie-boy?" Figo mumbled in his gravel-throated voice. Everyone in town knew this pint-sized sports promoter, a frequent caller to WKST radio's "Open Mike" and a local celebrity. Black-and-white signed photographs of sports stars and actors lined the walls of the shop.

"Hey, Frankie, they was just talking about you on the radio. They called you the devil man. What do you think?" Figo hoped to get a rise out of Costal.

Costal laughed, and Figo squinted as he put two fingers above his bald head.

"These are your devil horns." Mike roared in the background.

"See you kidders later." Costal waved to the barbers and headed through the alley to Towne Mall.

Left: Towne Mall. *Author's collection.*

Opposite: The Costal apartment. *Author's collection.*

Costal, who sometimes called himself Frank Batzel, located a bench and scouted the guys who walked past him. He maintained meticulous notes in his diary about his real and imaginary contacts. He referred to himself as a virgin since he had never slept with a woman. The mall seemed quiet. He bought some smokes and ambled to the Murphy's lunch bar for a cup of coffee.

Leaving the mall, he made his way to the art store on North Street for yarn to finish a string art project. He wove designs such as a Maltese cross with a Harley-Davidson cycle in its center, a high-masted sailboat or a chess knight on a handmade loom to sell in the projects. He also liked to paint. In fact, he sold his first painting to his friend Edith Coast for fifteen dollars.

After obtaining the yarn, he trudged back up the hill to his apartment at 1202 Highland Avenue. A stately yellow-brick exterior with white pillars masked the eerie interior of Costal's upstairs apartment, a shrine to the occult. In the living room, a voodoo doll with a head pierced by pins and a brain cavity charred black during a ritual stared into space above the mantel. A portrait of a cross-legged, goat-like Satan with elongated breasts, horns, a goatee and massive wings hung on one wall. His piercing red eyes

glared malevolently. The Latin word *Salve*, "salvation," was tattooed on the figure's right forearm. His hand clenched a pitchfork raised above his head. The beast's left hand pointed downward to hell. An upside-down crucifix with a skeleton hung on another wall, centered between a set of comedy and tragedy masks.

A third wall contained a pentagram with the name "Samael" emblazoned across the top and "Lilith" on the bottom. In Christianity, the five-pointed star symbolized mankind. The top point represented the head, the other four points the arms and legs. Satanism inverted the meaning. The top two points became Satan's horns and the bottom his tail, pointing downward to hell. Samael and Lilith were two demons. In Talmudic legend, the once beautiful Lilith had been a wife to Adam, but Samael, whose name means "Venom of God," seduced her, and she turned into a nocturnal fiend who preyed on children. Satanists considered Samael as the true father of Cain. Thus, when Cain slew his brother Abel, the crime involved the work of the devil, evil destroying good.

Costal interspersed religious icons and a picture of the Last Supper with satanic representations. He affixed plastic bats to his white lampshades and constructed an altar in the darkest corner of the room. Blood-red curtains draped the windows.

On special nights, Costal, clad in a high priest's robe with the Star of David emblazoned on the front and the four signs of life spread across

Comedy-tragedy masks
at the Costal apartment.
*Courtesy of the New Castle
Police Department.*

its back, performed wedding ceremonies, satanic masses or seances for his motley crew. He often read and interpreted passages from Anton Szandor LaVey's *Satanic Bible*, Gavin and Yvonne Frost's *Witches Bible* or David St. Clair's *Drum and Candle* for his clueless followers. He might chant in Enochian, a language thought to be older than Sanskrit, resembling Arabic in some sounds and Hebrew or Latin in others. Costal's intensity lifted his words: "Ol Sonief Vaoresaji gohu lad balita. In the name of Satan, I command the forces of darkness to bestow infernal power on me. So it is done." Thrusting a sword aloft, he would ring a bell nine times with his free hand to summon the forces of darkness. His audiences watched in silence, too absorbed to move, too terrified to respond. They lacked the mentality to separate Costal's carnival hoopla from reality. Like legendary promoter Phineas T. Barnum, the self-proclaimed warlock knew that a humbug was no humbug as long as the marks believed.

Costal frequented the New Castle Library's books on witchcraft, devil worship and cults. When a librarian refused his demand for immediate service, he placed a curse on her. The librarian laughed, but Costal took such curses seriously.

During evenings, he often turned to the writings of Anton Szandor LaVey, the father of the Church of Satan. Like Costal, LaVey's father had emigrated from Europe and eked out a marginal living. To escape

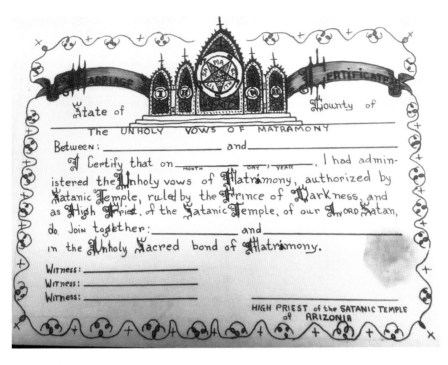

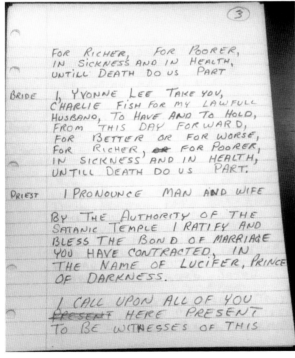

Above: Misspelled Satanic wedding certificate. *Courtesy of the New Castle Police Department.*

Left: A portion of the wedding ceremony. *Courtesy of the New Castle Police Department.*

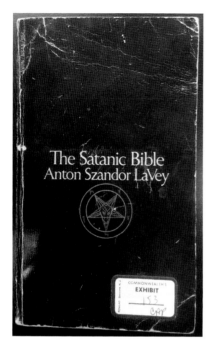

Left: The Satanic Bible, by Anton Szandor LaVey. *Courtesy of the New Castle Police Department.*

Right: Anton Szandor LaVey. *Courtesy of findagrave.com.*

an autocratic father, both dropped out of school and ran away to join the carnival, where they developed a fascination with the occult.

Costal and LaVey each possessed imposing physiques with strong features and penetrating eyes. However, Costal's long scraggly hair and wild unkempt beard contrasted with LaVey's shaved head and neatly trimmed goatee. Both relished the darkness. At night, Costal studied satanic books, practicing black magic or watching television until well after midnight. LaVey's seances lasted deep into the morning hours, and he slept in a coffin.

LaVey boasted of the power to curse his enemies and reward his friends. When a policeman pulled him over for a traffic infraction and disrespected him in front of a girlfriend, LaVey hexed the officer. Within hours, the policeman suffered a horrible accident. Likewise, when a taxi refused Costal entry, he cursed the driver, who later wrecked his car. Both men possessed prodigious sexual appetites—Costal for boys and men, LaVey for movie sirens such as Marilyn Monroe and Jayne Mansfield.

Other similarities abounded. The satanic symbols within Costal's apartment mimicked those found in LaVey's black Victorian mansion.

LaVey owned a pet lion, Tagore, Costal a parrot. LaVey was a top-notch painter and musician. Costal produced excellent weavings and painted quite well. Costal's nephew Bernard Laux even claimed to have met Californian Anton LaVey at the New Castle apartment, probably an idle boast.

Costal combined his art and homosexuality with beer, cigarettes, pot, television and the occult to carve out his bizarre lifestyle. He surrounded himself with drifters, druggies, criminals and misfits to bolster his self-importance. In the words of his mentor Anton LaVey: "Even though tricksters make the law, justice is served by fang and claw." Costal employed the black arts and a carny mentality as his fang and claw.

6

ATKINSON

Savoring the thrust of his fist slamming into the old man's jaw, Mike Atkinson smirked. A loud popping sound echoed through the bar as his unsuspecting victim dropped a bottle of beer and fell to his knees with a thud. A surprised look crossed his unshaven face. A gurgle drifted from his throat. Beer from the drunk's bottle spilled across the hardwood floor, forming an oval puddle. Without hesitating, Mike kicked his victim in the chest and watched him fold into a heap. A drop of blood trickled from the man's mouth. The force of the blow drove the empty bottle across the floor to shatter against the opposite wall. Mike gloated, his eyes locked in a malevolent glare. "Serves you right. I don't take no lip from some old rummy."

Atkinson viewed himself as a rock, a hitman for hire, a modern-day Billy the Kid, a scrapper, an underdog who fought to even the score. "Life ain't fair. When you're dealt a bum hand, you've got to pull an ace or two from up your sleeve if you want to win the pot."

Michael Robert Atkinson was born in Beaver Falls, a steel town neighboring New Castle, on October 6, 1951. Mike had a younger brother, Mark, and a sister, Billie, but folks dubbed Mike the bad apple of the lot. Since Mike made his own rules, those opinions meant nothing to him.

Mike grew up with a cruel streak, and that cruelty only increased with age. School bored him. Class work gave him fits, and the teachers cut him little slack. He dropped out in the eighth grade at the age of fourteen. He caught menial jobs in the Vanport area loading and unloading trucks for Greyhound or Northwestern Van Lines.

When off work, Atkinson floated in and out of trouble. The Beaver Falls police arrested him for malicious mischief when he was twenty. Six months later, they rearrested him for arson. While stoned on acid, he and an accomplice melted three railroad boxcars filled with fuel oil. Due to his youth and relatively clean police record, the judge sentenced him to six months of probation. Believing a transfer to a new community might be of benefit, the courts remanded him to a work-release program in Syracuse, New York, where he ground out a living as a laborer for a home improvement company.

On August 18, 1972, after his return from Syracuse, Mike married a girl named Dorothy from Wampum, a tiny burg located between Beaver Falls and New Castle. In 1974, the couple moved to Ellwood City, where Dorothy gave birth to a son, Michael Jr. The marriage proved rocky. The Atkinsons argued constantly, separating at the end of the year. However, they had a second son, Adam, born in 1975 after their divorce. Mike and his new girlfriend Leona Bullock had a daughter, Jennifer, the same year.

Atkinson found himself in trouble again while living in New Castle in early 1978. Ex-girlfriend Darlene Pounds told friends he held a knife against her throat and beat her. Pounds refused to stand by and be manhandled a second time. When Atkinson pointed a pistol at her head from inside his station wagon, she pressed charges. Mike pleaded guilty to a misdemeanor.

Atkinson hung out with a crew of thugs and misfits. Sometimes, he strapped a fishing knife to his hip, just in case. One of Mike's more interesting pals was Satanist and homosexual Frank Costal, with whom he had experienced a tumble or two in the hay, although Mike far preferred rough-and-tumble sex with the ladies.

A woman reported in a police interview: "He slapped me around and said he was going to rape me if I didn't cooperate. He became violent and bit me on the breast and left marks there. He then performed oral sex on me and said he liked to do this when I was bleeding. Then, he performed anal sex on me. After that I did not go near Mike anymore."

Mike's crudeness repulsed most women. His dark eyes projected the iciness of a ravenous shark hunting prey. Although only five feet, eight inches, he possessed a powerful frame coupled with a heartless soul. A swarthy face and a slight bend in his once-broken nose amplified his ominous look. His familiarity with Satanism scared off another girlfriend when he told her he could "kill a man without touching him, because he knows someone with supernatural powers," an obvious allusion to Costal.

On September 5, 1978, Atkinson and a mentally challenged twenty-three-year-old, Raymond Thompson, abducted a sixteen-year-old girl who had been dating Thompson's younger brother, Ron. When Ron went into a store to buy cigarettes, Atkinson took off with the juvenile and drove to Medusa Lake near Wampum, where he raped the girl at knifepoint while his friend watched. When he finished, Atkinson forced Raymond to rape her as well. Atkinson threatened to kill the sobbing girl if she told anyone. She swore an oath of silence to save her life. The men drove to New Castle and dropped her off downtown.

Once free, the victim ran to the police, who arrested Raymond Thompson the following morning. Thompson pleaded guilty to aggravated assault and received a sentence in January 1979 for a three-to-eight-year stretch at Rockview Penitentiary in Bellefonte.

When two state policemen appeared at Atkinson's home to arrest him, Mike begged for permission to go back inside to retrieve his five-year-old son. The officer in charge agreed, and Atkinson escaped through the back door with the boy in tow.

Atkinson called his friend Costal and asked him to meet at the Burger Chef. "Frank, I've got big trouble with the law. I need to leave town fast. You know the wife and me split. She was just a whore anyhow. Since she left, I've been looking after Mike Jr. I want you to take him for a couple of weeks until things calm down. If you do, I'll make it worth your while when I return. I got a stash hidden away, and I'll share it with you."

"Mike, I can't take no kid. I wouldn't know what do with him."

Atkinson rose to his feet and glared. "I won't forget this, you queer son-of-a-bitch." He grabbed his son's hand and stormed out of the restaurant, forcing the boy on his ex-wife. Mike Atkinson would harbor a grudge against Costal for some time.

Mike skipped out to Syracuse, living under the radar of the law. He disguised his appearance to avoid detection. He grew a beard and wore his hair long. Adding 70 pounds to his frame, his weight ballooned to 250.

By early 1980, Atkinson assumed police pressure had cooled. On January 7, he sneaked into Ellwood City using the aliases "Mike Bell" and "Mike Italia." His father, John Atkinson, helped him lease a second-floor apartment at 422 Franklin Avenue from landlord John McCurdy. The father explained that his son had just returned from Syracuse and was waiting for a check that would arrive in a few days. The landlord agreed to cooperate.

Mike Bell moved in with a handful of possessions. To bring in a few bucks, he subleased the unfinished third-floor attic above his room to William Owens, a nomad he met at the Oasis Bar. He pocketed the rent and held off paying McCurdy the money he owed.

Around four o'clock in the afternoon of January 16, clad in a dirty T-shirt, worn jeans and a wool-lined jean jacket, Atkinson sauntered into the Oasis Bar in downtown Ellwood. Rapping on the counter for attention, he ordered a whiskey and a Miller High Life from bartender Berniece Annabella. Atkinson chugged the whiskey, following it with the beer chaser.

"Hey, Berniece, how's about another?" Atkinson spat into a nearby ashtray.

Following a few more swigs, Atkinson slurred his words and rambled semi-coherently. He mumbled half-aloud, "Need some dollars quick or I'm out on the streets."

Mike was broke. His landlord had threatened to evict him for nonpayment of rent. Atkinson tried to stall, but McCurdy refused to bite. He needed cash, and he needed it fast. Then, he remembered the old woman, Rosie Puz, in the apartment beneath his. He had used her telephone a couple of times since he couldn't afford one of his own. She appeared well fixed. He remembered seeing the old woman's collection of silver and gold coins on her dresser—plus, her TV and appliances could come in handy.

Mrs. Puz kept to herself and looked frail, couldn't weigh much more than one hundred pounds soaking wet, and best of all, she lived alone. Mike grinned. The old lady seemed ripe for the picking.

"You want another?" The bartender asked, spotting Atkinson's empty glasses. He usually drank sparingly, opting for dope rather than booze. Berniece thought he looked nervous. "Everything okay?"

"Yea, sure. Just one more beer, and I got to go."

He took his drink and walked to the pay phone to call his mother. He knew better than to try his father. "Mom, I am tapped. Can you help me out?" When his mother refused, he slammed the phone to the receiver. He stormed back to his stool to finish his beer. Within minutes, he calmed down.

"Hey, Berniece."

"Yeah."

"If you ever need household stuff like candlesticks or appliances, just let me know, okay?"

"Sure," the bartender answered. She could outfit a castle if she bought all the hot goods offered to her.

At five o'clock, Atkinson left the Oasis.

Around 5:45 p.m., Hilda Balmini, a neighbor of Rosie Puz's, spotted a cream-colored station wagon parked in front of the 422 Franklin Avenue apartment. At seven o'clock in the evening, George VanSickle, a retired schoolteacher who lived next door to Mrs. Puz, returned home carrying groceries. As he stopped to balance the bags in his arms, he noticed Mike

Bell's father standing by a station wagon. He caught sight of a lampshade in the back along with stacks of household goods.

At 12:15 that night, another neighbor, Mrs. DeRosa, smelled something burning. She peeked out her window and saw smoke pouring from the Puz apartment. She telephoned the Ellwood City Police, who dispatched Officer Joseph DeSanzo, the acting turn lieutenant, to investigate. He radioed the fire station to get to the scene on the double.

The high-pitched blare of sirens screamed through the Ellwood City streets, stopping abruptly at 422 Franklin. Officer DeSanzo smashed the front door window with his flashlight. A volunteer fireman reached his gloved hand inside and turned the knob. Firefighters wearing Scott air packs streamed through the smoke-filled entrance while a pumper truck doused the roof with water.

The telltale signs of arson became obvious. The perpetrators lit a fire in the kitchen and a second in the living room. They piled sheets and blankets around the perimeter to build the heat level. Evidence indicated the fires had been set sometime between six and eight o'clock earlier that evening.

Fireman Don Reid found the contents of the house scattered haphazardly. Drawers had been overturned and the contents dumped. The intruders emptied closets and tossed the clothing in a pile in the corner. They ransacked tables and chairs and flung lamps to the side. The television stand lay empty.

Inside the kitchen, glass from smashed dishes crunched beneath the firemen's boots as they tramped across the floor. Most of the kitchen pots and pans appeared to be missing.

Reid scoured through the living room debris and picked up what looked like a part of a mannequin from a hole in the floor. Upon closer examination, the thing resembled the charred remains of a human arm. Shining his flashlight into the six-by-four hole made by the fire, he shouted: "Someone get over here. We have a body."

A ray of light from the flashlight bounced off the shape of a horribly mutilated human form. The paper-thin remains of Rosie Puz lay suspended across a wooden beam. The right arm was contorted, the left severed below the elbow. A shattered lower leg dangled by a few stringy tendons. Heat from the flames consumed the victim's hair and face. The boiling fluids in the victim's brain expanded and burst through the skull.

Fireman Patterson inspected the kitchen. The burners of the gas stove had been turned to the "on" position. He shut off the burners. A melted candle sat in the center of the room, a small portion of the wick intact. Only a lack of oxygen saved the house from a massive explosion.

After almost an hour, the firefighters contained the fire. A full arson and homicide investigation began in earnest. A state trooper scouted the scene for clues. He theorized that clothing and sheets had been piled on top of Mrs. Puz's body after the fire had been set.

At 1:10 a.m., the Lawrence County deputy coroner examined Rosie Volk Puz's remains. An ambulance with a driver and two assistants placed the body of the eighty-four-year-old victim in a body bag and drove to the Allegheny County Morgue for an autopsy. Since the case looked like a homicide, police cordoned off the apartment to protect the crime scene and questioned the neighbors. When the authorities learned a man named Michael Bell lived in the apartment above Mrs. Puz, they placed him at the top of the list for questioning.

The following morning, the police searched the crime scene and dusted for fingerprints. They uncovered a plain white envelope containing $1,087 in cash beneath the kitchen sink, missed by the robber/arsonists.

Sometime between 7:30 and 8:00 p.m. the night of the fire, John Atkinson drove his son to the home of Tom and Connie Hall in nearby Eastvale, located in Beaver County. The Halls had just put their three young children to bed and were watching television with a cousin, Ronald Bennett. A rap on the door interrupted them.

"Coming," answered Connie.

"Hey, Connie, the wife and me split, and I just got back from New York. I ain't got no place to stay. Can I come in?" Mike asked.

Connie Hall, an oversized, bighearted lady, remembered Mike from the days when both of them lived in the ramshackle apartments at Crescentdale outside Wampum. Although she always distrusted Atkinson, she was reluctant to turn away anyone in need.

"Sure, come on in, Mike." She pointed to a dark red spot on the chest of his shirt. "What's that?"

"Nothing, you ought to see the other guy." Mike brushed off the question. "Listen, I got a TV set for you and Tom if you put me up for a couple of days. What do you say?"

"Why not! Tom isn't working, and we don't have much in the way of food, but you can stay a while."

Mike hauled a television and a bushel basket of clothes into the living room and deposited the stuff on the floor in the corner.

After some chitchat with Connie about Crescentdale, Mike turned to Tom and asked, "If a lighted candle had been set in a room with natural gas coming from a stove, how long would you think it would take to explode?"

"Beats me," answered Tom. "I guess it would depend on the size of the room. Why?"

"Just curious," Mike responded.

Following the eleven o'clock news and some more chitchat, the Halls headed to their bedroom, leaving Mike to sleep on the couch.

The next morning, Mike's father returned with four or five cardboard boxes filled with household goods. Mike and his dad unloaded them onto the porch. After John Atkinson's departure, Mike and Tom carried the stuff into the house, where they looked over the loot. They sorted through Christmas decorations, a Sunbeam toaster, a pressure cooker, wall plaques, a glass pitcher, a camera, dustpans, flatware, two General Electric irons, assorted clothing and jewelry. Mike and Tom separated the most salable items: a lady's Timex watch, earrings, gold jewelry, a Sound Design radio, a Spartan wall clock, a K-Mart fan, dishes, pots and pans. Mike needed money, so he selected several pieces to sell.

Tom started his old Dodge van and drove Mike to a pawn shop in Monaca, a small town just six miles from Beaver Falls. Mike sold a ring, a gold chain, a pair of earrings and some dental gold for twenty dollars. He pocketed most of the cash, slipping Tom a few dollars for gas. After a bite to eat, the men headed to John Brown's antique store in New Brighton, but the portly owner refused to make an offer.

That night, Mike asked Tom for a haircut. "Why don't you just shave my whole head?" Tom obliged before turning in for the night.

Mike remained with the Halls all day Friday, January 18, selling a set of flatware to Connie's sister for fifteen dollars. On the nineteenth, Tom drove Mike to New Galilee to visit Linda Clemmer O'Neil, another Crescentdale acquaintance. After gabbing about the old neighborhood, Mike asked if he could stay for a few days. Linda agreed.

On the twenty-first, Connie sat on her couch and scanned the *Ellwood City Ledger*. The price of gold had leapt to $875 per ounce, but the headline really smacked her in the head: "POLICE SEEK RESIDENT OF SECOND FLOOR ROOM." As Connie digested the article, she recognized the mess facing Tom and her.

"Tom, listen to this story in the paper":

> *Ellwood city police are looking for Michael Atkinson, also known as Mike Bell and Mike Italia, 28, of 422 Franklin Avenue, for questioning in the possible murder, arson and robbery of the late Rosie Volk Puz, who burned to death in her apartment last Thursday. Police said they want him for questioning because evidence indicates that Mrs. Puz may have died as a*

result of possible homicide by arson with robbery as the motive. Atkinson was a tenant in the same house as Mrs. Puz and was last seen Tuesday, but now has disappeared without a trace. Police said Atkinson is 5'8" tall and weighs between 250 and 280 pounds. He is also wanted by the state police who hold a fugitive warrant for his arrest. The man sought for questioning has dark brown hair and a mustache as well as a scraggly short beard. He has brown eyes according to police, who warned he may be armed with a small caliber pistol. Anyone with information about Atkinson-Bell is asked to contact police at 758-9905. Any information will be held in confidence, and no source will be revealed, police said.

"Holy Christ!" Tom shouted. Although Tom had only a fifth-grade education, he knew that he had helped Mike pawn stolen merchandise. The Halls had to get Atkinson out of the house and contact the police.

Atkinson continued to sell his swag. He offered a copper pot to Cosmo Geniviva at the Oasis Bar for a price. Geniviva declined but suggested he try Jul's Auto Repairs in Burnstown, where he sold it for fifteen dollars. Later that afternoon, Mike gathered some of his belongings and placed them in Tom's van. He agreed to pick up the remainder later in the week. The Halls dropped Mike off at Linda O'Neill's and hurried home to phone the police and let them know where Atkinson could be found.

Linda's father and her brothers were sitting in the living room when Mike arrived. The group chatted until around 10:00 p.m., when Linda answered a banging on the door. Two uniformed state troopers barreled into the room, one with a pistol drawn and the other hefting a shotgun. They stared directly at Atkinson.

"Are you Michael Atkinson?"

"Hey, there's no need to hassle me with them guns," Atkinson replied, raising his hands.

The police ordered him to move against the wall, where they searched for weapons before handcuffing him. Linda and her family watched in confusion.

"What's going on?" asked one of Linda's brothers. The police ignored the question.

"Okay, let's go outside." An officer read Mike his rights and advised him he was being held on a fugitive rape warrant and suspicion of murder. The officers hauled him to the state police barracks for processing before depositing him in the Lawrence County Jail.

Lieutenant Jack Maine of the Ellwood City Police drove to the Halls' home after Atkinson was booked to pick up any remaining possessions as

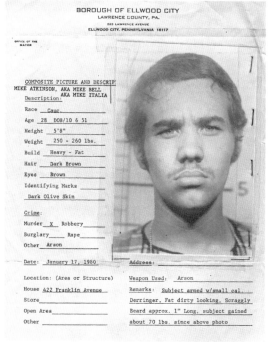

Above: Mike Atkinson's booking photo. *Courtesy of the New Castle Police Department.*

Left: Mike Atkinson's rap sheet. *Courtesy of the New Castle Police Department.*

Opposite: Mike Atkinson's fingerprints. *Courtesy of the New Castle Police Department.*

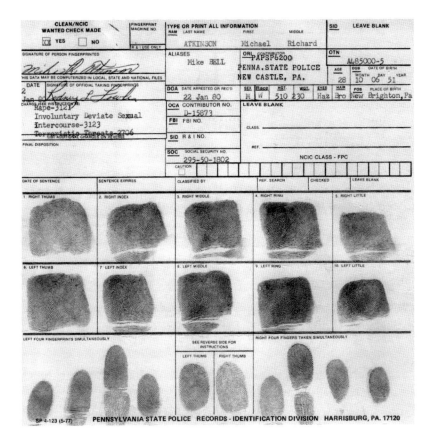

evidence. After questioning them, he gave the Halls a $800 receipt for the household goods and informed them that they were suspects. They protested their innocence and promised to cooperate.

"Don't leave town. We will want to talk to you again," Maine warned.

During Mike's first day in jail, two policemen came to his cell with a search warrant for pubic hairs and blood. Mike played the tough guy role.

"I'm in a lousy mood. You can stick it where the sun don't shine as far as I am concerned."

"Listen, Atkinson. You're here on charges of robbery, theft, arson, receiving stolen property, deviant sexual behavior and who knows what else. Things might just go a little better if you play ball with us."

Mike groused but went to the hospital for testing.

In jail, Mike became known as "Mr. Complainer" to the guards. The other prisoners considered him a blowhard and a liar. Soon, Mike's big mouth would land him in even deeper trouble.

7

THE PLOT THICKENS

Detective Bureau," Leon Sasiadek answered the phone.

"You got a guy named Atkinson in the Lawrence County Jail?" a female voice asked.

"Who is calling, please?"

"That ain't important. Just listen for a minute. Before you put Atkinson in the slammer, he shot off his mouth about some lady and her kid who was killed a while back. I don't take to no baby killers. You might want to look into this."

"Hold on please." Sasiadek called across the room: "Hey Gig, you'd better get on the line—now!"

Detective Frank Gagliardo picked up a second phone and jotted down the informant's information. She lived on Long Avenue and sounded reliable. This was the department's first lead on the Kadunce killings in nearly eighteen months.

"Hey Chuck," Gig called to Detective Charles Abraham after hanging up the phone. "Do you know the name Mike Atkinson?"

"I think I do—big mouth, a bully. Why?" Back when Abraham was working narcotics, Atkinson had provided him with some intel, none of which proved useful.

"We just got a tip Atkinson might know something about the Kadunce murders."

"Where is he?"

"Lawrence County Jail. Maybe you can pay him a visit?" Gig asked.

"Sure, I'll head over after work."

Around 6:00 p.m., Abraham met with Atkinson in the medical cell at the jail. The room, barely large enough for a table and two chairs, felt tight, and the detective disliked tight places. Atkinson paced to and fro like a caged tiger, his eyes darting from side to side.

"What do you want?"

"Mike, why don't you just take a seat?"

The prisoner sat without objection. Abraham knew little about the Kadunce case, but he acted as if he had more info than he did.

"Hi Mike, you remember me?

Atkinson nodded.

"I understand you know a lot about the Kadunce killings?"

Atkinson grinned like an eight-year-old caught by his parents in a lie.

"I wasn't there," he stammered, "but the husband was involved."

"Don't mess with me. He took a lie detector test and passed." Actually, the results proved inconclusive, but neither Abraham nor Atkinson knew that.

"Well, I wasn't there, but I heard who was. Frank Costal, Jim Antoniotti, and his wife, Judy. They was there and used a plastic runner on the stairs to keep the blood off the floor."

"Mike, is there anything else you can tell me?"

"No, that's all I heard. I don't know nothing else."

"Okay thanks, Mike. Let me know if you can think of anything else. I'll be back."

Abraham left the jail, got in his car and drove home. The interview gnawed at him along the way. Atkinson knew more than he was saying. After dinner, he called Gig.

"This guy mentioned a plastic runner on the steps to cover up bloodstains and named names. I know he's up to his ears involved. I need to read up on the case."

"Okay, Babe. Tomorrow we can go over the files."

The following morning, Abraham and Gagliardo went over the facts. Blood covered the walls and floor of the bathroom and Dawn's bedroom. The steps were clean. Atkinson's story of a plastic runner made sense.

"Gig, I'm going to pay another visit to the jail. I am pretty sure he was in the house the day of the murders. I'm going to push him hard to see what I can get."

That afternoon, Abraham made a second trip to the jail.

"Mike, we've got to talk some more about the Kadunce case. What do you think the inmates here will do when they hear you were involved in the murder of a four-year-old child? They don't like child killers, do they?"

"I didn't do nothing to no kid."

"Mike, I know you were there." Abraham emphasized the word *know*. After a spot of silence, Mike spoke.

"Yeah, but I didn't do nothing. I stayed in the car the whole time. Them other guys done it, and I can deliver Costal to you on a silver platter. You just got to move me out of this place if you want me alive to testify."

"Okay, Mike, that's it for now. Don't say anything to anyone. Understand?" Mike nodded his head in agreement. Abraham planned to come back in a day or two with a witness and a tape recorder.

Back at the detective bureau, Abraham met with Gig and Chief Joe Farris, Carbone's replacement.

"He sang like a bird. We have him."

"Let's pick up Antoniotti," chimed in Gig. "We'll see what he has to say." Antoniotti had proven helpful to the police in the past. He had also served time for burglarizing Pete's Bait Shop.

On February 9, 1980, the police picked up Antoniotti and dragged him to the city building for questioning. Antoniotti was a wiry, catlike man in his thirties with short hair and a quick temper. The cops strong-armed him into coming clean. After the necessary "encouragement," he confessed to being at the Kadunce home the day of the murder. The case began to look like a slam dunk. Abraham conferred with District Attorney Don Williams and prepared the following affidavit of probable cause against Frank George Costal Jr.:

Charles Abraham of the New Castle police department, being duly sworn according to law, says that probable cause exists for the issuance of a process based on the following facts and circumstances.

James Antoniotti of 531 Electric Street, New Castle, Pa., came to the detective bureau of the New Castle police department this date and advised your affiant that on the morning Kathy Kadunce had been found dead in her home at 702 Wilmington Avenue, he and his wife Judy had gone to the parking lot of the Fast 'n Friendly store adjacent to the residence of Kathy Kadunce as passengers in a blue Mustang driven by Michael Atkinson and in which Frank George Costal, Jr. was a passenger in the right seat. He related that Atkinson parked the vehicle in the Fast 'n Friendly parking lot, and Atkinson and Costal went up to the front door of the Kadunce residence and went inside about one-half hour, and when they came out Atkinson had blood all over his trousers, arm, sleeve and hand, and Costal had blood on his hands and fingers. That after getting in the car, both Atkinson and Costal told Antoniotti and his wife Judy that if they ever said anything to anybody about "this," they would be shot or knifed, that Atkinson drove down Canyon Street from the Fast 'n Friendly parking lot and by that route to 387 Halco Drive, where Antoniotti and his wife were dropped off, and Atkinson said they had to "get rid of something" and drove away.

Antoniotti related further that upon getting out of the Mustang at the Fast 'n Friendly parking lot Atkinson had a big hunting knife on his side in a holder of some kind, but on coming out he did not have the knife, that he, Antoniotti, was familiar with Atkinson carrying a knife, and Atkinson had previously threatened him with the same knife and shook it in his face.

Antoniotti stated he had known both Atkinson and Costal for a considerable time before this event in July of 1978, and also he had known Kathy Kadunce many months before July, 1978, and had been to her apartment prior to this by himself, and also his wife was acquainted with Kathy Kadunce for a period of time before that date.

James Antoniotti has been known by your affiant for several years and has been known by District Attorney Donald E. Williams for several years, who stated James Antoniotti has furnished him information which led to the conviction of defendants previously. Your affiant was also informed by Frank Gagliardo that he has known James Antoniotti and deems the said James Antoniotti to be reliable.

Antoniotti also related he has known Costal since he was a boy. He knew Costal has two guns in his apartment in a cupboard in the rear thereof, and he has seen the apartment and is familiar with it, and Costal has talked to him many times of the two guns he owns, where he keeps them, and he knew how to use them. Also, he revealed that Atkinson and Costal, before going to 702 Wilmington Avenue that morning, told Antoniotti they were going to "get even with that bitch," and at the time they were talking about Kathy Kadunce.

Wherefore, your affiant believes Frank George Costal, Jr. did participate in the murder of Kathy Kadunce on the 11th day of July, 1978, and he did accomplish said crime, in part, by using a firearm which he did keep in his apartment at 1202 Highland Avenue, and by reason of his still residing there that said firearm is at said premises, and the knife or sharp instruments utilized in said crime are probably kept with said firearm, we request the issuance of a warrant for the arrest of Frank Costal, Jr. for criminal homicide and request the issuance of a search warrant for a daytime search of the apartment of Frank Costal, Jr. for any evidence which will relate Costal to the murder of Kathy Kadunce.

Sworn to and subscribed before me this 9th day of February, 1980, by Sgt. Charles Abraham, New Castle Police Department

Mike Atkinson's blue Mustang. *Courtesy of the New Castle Police Department.*

Abraham worried that Atkinson's and Antoniotti's confessions might leak out to Costal. "We'd better act fast. We can get Atkinson's written statement later. We don't want Costal skipping on us."

After District Attorney Williams rechecked the wording of the affidavit, Gig phoned District Justice Howard "Coffee" Hanna, who although off duty, agreed to issue the warrant for Costal's arrest that very afternoon.

"You guys pick me up, and we'll take care of the paperwork at the office," the district magistrate mumbled. Coffee liked having the police pick him up, even though his Ray Street home stood only a few blocks from his Washington Street office.

At the station, Gig asked Abraham to handle the paperwork. He would get Keys and execute the arrest. "We can stay in touch by radio. I won't do anything until I know the paperwork is complete. We don't want problems over some technicality."

While Chuck picked up Hanna, Gig and Keys hopped into an unmarked Plymouth and headed up Highland to survey Costal's apartment. A neighbor advised them Costal had left.

"Maybe he's at Burger Chef. I hear he hangs out there," Gig suggested. Costal was not there.

"Let's check Towne Mall," Gig offered. Again, no luck. "I'd better call Chuck and see how he's doing. We can use the phone at the Post Office Lunch."

Gig called Coffee Hanna's office and spoke to Abraham. "We can't find him anywhere. Sure hope he hasn't fled the coop."

"Hope not. I've run into a little snag. We forgot to include the little girl in the affidavit. She should have been included so we can file charges on two counts of murder instead of one. It's going to take me a little longer than I thought."

"Holy cow," Gig interrupted, eying the unmistakable shape of Costal walking outside the window. He nudged Keys. "Do you see what I see?" Keys nodded. "Chuck, speaking of the devil, he is walking past the restaurant right now. He's heading to the mall. Rush those warrants along for us. Gotta go. We'll keep in touch over the radio."

"We'll move as fast as we can, but need a little more time," Chuck answered. "Good luck."

Gig adjusted the squelch on his portable radio to tune out extraneous noise and followed Costal to the mall. Costal stopped at the game room, staring at the kids playing the video machines. The flashing lights mesmerized the big man. While Keys kept Costal in sight, Gig phoned Chuck from Mr. Pizza across the hall.

"We're on him like white on rice. He's in the game room. How are you coming?"

"Need a few more minutes. We'll be done soon."

"Okay, sure hope he doesn't bolt," Gig interjected. Keys motioned from across the hall. "Gotta go, he's on the move."

Costal walked out the main entrance of the mall toward the bus stop. Climbing aboard, he sat in the center of the nearly empty vehicle. Gig and Keys followed. The female bus driver, who recognized the plainclothes detectives, blurted out: "Well, what do we have here, a police convention?"

Gig scowled and put his finger to his lips, hoping the comment hadn't spooked Costal. The driver ceased further recognition. Gig moved to the back of the bus to block Costal from leaving through the rear door. Keys sat down toward the front.

Reaching beneath his jacket, Gig removed his walkie-talkie. He bent behind the seat and whispered: "Can you read me?"

"Loud and clear."

"We're on the bus with our boy. Any progress?"

"Coffee's almost done."

"Well, get to it. I'll call back in a few minutes."

When the bus stopped in front of the Strauss Department Store at the corner of Highland and North Streets minutes later, Gagliardo cued the driver. "Wait for me. I'll be right back."

Gig walked behind the bus. Bending on his haunches while trying to appear inconspicuous, Gig called Chuck. "Got the papers?"

"All set. We have the warrant. Let's meet in front of Costal's apartment and arrest him there. See you in a couple of minutes."

Gagliardo switched off the radio and tucked it under his jacket before reentering the bus. As he walked toward his seat, he winked at Keys. Leaning back, he noticed the bus was turning on North Street rather than proceeding up Highland. He hoped Abraham would realize this bus took a slightly different route.

Chief Joe Farris left Coffee Hanna's office with the district attorney in the front seat and Abraham and Lastoria in the back. The four parked in front of Costal's yellow-brick apartment at 1202 Highland and awaited Keys and Gagliardo. The minutes dragged like hours.

"We didn't pass the bus on the way. Shouldn't it be here by now?" Chief Farris asked.

"You're right," Williams agreed, checking his watch.

"Chief," Abraham chimed in, "I think some of the buses go up Wilmington to Clen-Moore. They turn on Mercer until they hit Englewood. I live on Englewood, and some of the buses take that route. Maybe we should check it out?"

"Good idea," the chief decided. As the car reached Englewood, the chief spotted the bus. The unmarked police car followed back down Highland until the bus stopped across the street from Costal's apartment. Costal exited first, followed by Keys and Gagliardo. The unmarked police car emptied, and Abraham, as the lead officer, approached Costal first. His hand instinctively reached for his thirty-eight special—just in case. With Costal outnumbered six to one, a weapon seemed unnecessary.

"Frank Costal?"

Costal faced the detective, and a quizzical expression crossed his face.

"You are under arrest for suspicion of murder." Abraham clicked the Smith and Wesson handcuffs across the prisoner's wrists. A thoroughly befuddled Costal gawked from one cop to the next. "Lieutenant Gagliardo, read him his rights."

Abraham walked to the car, reached in and grabbed the police radio. "This is Abraham. Do you read me?"

A voice over the radio grunted affirmatively.

"Send a marked car and a detective car to 1202 Highland on the double." The patrol car would alert the neighbors that a formal investigation was in process.

Abraham returned to face the prisoner. "Mr. Costal, we have a search warrant for your apartment. We'd like you to go with us."

Costal made no attempt to answer. He silently accompanied the authorities across the street to his second-floor apartment. As the police entered the living room, Gagliardo, a practicing Catholic, exclaimed: "Holy Mother of God." Plastic black bats on the lampshades, ruby-red candles and a satanic altar blanketed with skulls greeted him. Poised on a psychedelic light sat a large skull with a bullet in its teeth and a wooden dagger slashing through the brain cavity. Blood-red curtains darkened the windows, and an inverted crucifix gilded with a skeleton menaced the ambiance. A picture of Satan pointing toward hell sent shivers among the trespassers into Costal's realm.

From the rear of the room, a piercing shriek erupted. Keys grabbed his pistol and turned to meet the nameless squawker, uncertain who or what monstrosity he would face. There perched in a cage sat Costal's pet parrot. Keys holstered his weapon. Gig and Chuck laughed mercilessly to ease the tension.

It was nearly 6:00 p.m. The police searched for the murder weapon and other incriminating evidence. Abraham confiscated two boxes of .25-caliber ammunition, an address book, Costal's diary and an album of photographs. Sergeant Abraham handed Costal a numbered receipt for the seized property.

"Gig, let's wrap this up. What do you think?"

"Sure. Let's take Frankie boy to the station, book him and send him off to jail." Gig nudged Costal. "Big day. Anything you want to tell us?" Costal ignored the jibe and stared blankly at the floor.

"What's a matter, cat got your tongue?" Gig nudged Costal again. The arrestee remained silent.

"Okay, let's get him in the cruiser," Abraham interrupted. "The search is over for tonight."

The detectives led Costal to the basement of the city building for processing. After fingerprinting, weighing and photographing the noncommunicative prisoner, the detectives drove Costal to the district magistrate's office for arraignment and on to the Lawrence County Jail. A uniformed guard escorted him to his cell. A buzzer rang. The metal gate clanged open. The manacled prisoner entered begrudgingly, his head sagging and shoulders drooping. Costal looked old.

Satanism book cover at the Costal apartment. *Courtesy of the New Castle Police Department.*

Frank Costal booking photo. *Courtesy of the New Castle Police Department.*

After a thorough search, Costal entered the general population to the catcalls of the already incarcerated. "Looks like some new meat, but it sure don't look fresh," called out one inmate. Others silently gawked at the strange-looking newcomer.

Costal ignored the hubbub. He sat on a wooden bench with his head in his hands.

On February 10, with Costal in the Lawrence County Jail, Sergeants Lastoria and Abraham drove to the Butler Jail, where Atkinson had been removed for his own protection. Mike provided the same basic testimony given earlier, but the details shifted. Atkinson agreed to allow Abraham to tape his statement.

The following day, after receiving a list of dos and don'ts from District Attorney Williams, Lastoria and Abraham returned to the Butler County Jail with the required waiver-of-rights forms and a tape recorder. The three men sat at a spartan table in the conference room. Atkinson rose as though about to object.

"Mike, sit down. We want to start." Atkinson sat, and Abraham adjusted the microphone.

"Mike, my name is Sergeant Charles Abraham, sitting with me is Sergeant Mike Lastoria. You know this conversation is being taped."

"Yes," Atkinson replied.

"Okay, what is your name?" Mike answered.

"How old are you?"

"Twenty-eight."

"Where do you live?"

"457 River Road. Vanport, Pennsylvania."

"Before we get started, I will advise you of your rights, okay?" Abraham read Atkinson his Miranda rights as prescribed by law. "Okay, do you understand all the rights I read to you?"

"Yes."

"Okay, having those rights in mind, do you want to talk to us now?"

"Yes," Mike answered.

"What we want to talk about is the murder of Kathy Kadunce and her daughter, Dawn, who lived at 702 Wilmington Avenue. The murder took place July 11, 1978."

"Right."

"Are you familiar with that?"

"Yes."

"Okay, what do you know about it?"

"Well, the night before it happened there was Jim Antoniotti, Judy Antoniotti, some kid named Paul, Paul Pounds, Kathy's sister, a girl named Bobbi and I, and we was all sitting around and…"

"Where were you at?" Abraham interrupted.

"Halco Drive at Jim Antoniotti's House."

"Okay."

"And we were talking, because we were waiting for an order of windowpane acid coming in, and Judy and Jim Antoniotti stated that Kathy ripped us off for the acid."

"Kathy who?"

"Kadunce," Atkinson answered. "She had to get rid of it because she was afraid of getting busted. So then Judy Antoniotti says it could have been Kathy that turned us in for our insurance deal. So Bobbi popped up and says, 'Tomorrow, somebody has to go up there and kick her rear end or threaten her for our acid,' and they arranged transportation through me. I was driving a '71 avocado-green station wagon that belonged to Darlene Miller and about…early in the morning…"

"What is the nearest time you can fix?"

"Well, I stayed at my house….At the time I was staying at 1315 South Jefferson with Darlene Miller. She was still sleeping when I left. It was about 6:45 in the morning, and I went up to 1202 Highland Avenue, picked up Frank."

"Frank who?"

"I know him by Basket or Basketwoods. I don't know how you pronounce it. And we left there and went over to Jim and Judy Antoniotti's house."

"This Frank, would he be Frank Costal? Did he go by that name, too?"

"Yes."

"Okay, go ahead."

"We left from the house. We crossed over from Highland to South State Street…no…yes, that's State Street, isn't that, at the top of the hill there by the police department."

"That's Wallace."

"Wallace?"

"Yes."

Atkinson continued. "Okay, I went the back way past Fast 'n Friendly, where Kathy Kadunce lived and down over the hill to Halco Drive. We picked up Jim Antoniotti, Judy Antoniotti and Paul."

"What's Paul's last name? Do you know it?"

"Not offhand."

"Okay, who sat where?"

"Frank was in the front. Jim and Paul was in the back seat. The understanding was…"

"Who was driving?"

"I was. The understanding was that Judy and I stay in the car while Frank, Jim and Paul went into the house. They was going to bounce her around and scare her to tell where she put the windowpane acid. They went in for about twenty minutes or half an hour, then Frank came out."

"Wait a minute. You're going too fast."

Atkinson paused. "I pulled up to Fast 'n Friendly, and I went in. I got myself a cup of coffee, and I got Judy a cup while Frank, Jim and Paul was over talking to Kathy."

"How do you know they were over there?"

"Because you could see from the car."

"Did you see them go in?"

"They went in the front door."

"Did you see any of them carrying any kind of weapon?"

"Paul always carries a hunting knife if you want to call it that. Some people call it a bayonet."

"How big was it?"

"The blade on it went about ten inches long."

"How wide?"

"About three quarters of an inch."

"Okay, go ahead."

"And they went in, a few minutes…not a few minutes, about twenty minutes to half an hour. Jim Antoniotti, Frank and Paul came out. When Paul came out, he didn't have his T-shirt on."

"Did you see anything unusual about them? Were they nervous, in a hurry, were they just walking normal or what?"

"They were walking normal when they came out. I noticed Paul didn't have his T-shirt on. He had his Levi jacket on. When I asked where his T-shirt was, he didn't say, so I noticed Frank's jacket. He had like blood or something on it. I says, 'What is that on your arm?' He said, 'Red paint.'"

"Did he have it on before he went in?"

"No, he didn't."

"You sure of that?"

"Yes."

"Did it look like red paint?"

"No, it looked like blood."

"Did anyone else have any of that…what looked like blood on them?"

"No. I asked Frank, I said, 'You sure it's paint not blood?' And he says, 'It's paint.' So I asked him what did they do while in there. They discussed it with Kathy, and Paul was supposed to smack Kathy around, him and Jim Antoniotti, and Kathy was supposed to have told Jim where the acid was, because that night Jim Antoniotti came over with the acid."

"Let's go back to when they got into the car. Was there any discussion as to what happened inside the house?"

"Just that Kathy was roughed up."

"Then what?"

"We left, and Jim Antoniotti said he had to go to the scrap yard to take cast iron in. I don't know if he went."

"When you left, which way did you go?"

"Down through Jim Antoniotti's, the same way we came."

"What time did you get to Jim Antoniotti's house?"

"About twenty to eight. I dropped Jim and Judy and Paul Antoniotti off. Frank wanted to go downtown to check his mailbox so I dropped him off downtown."

"When did you first learn a murder had happened at the house?"

"About a week later I found out about it, because after I was up there, I was into a family feud with the Pounds and the Millers, and I had to protect…"

"Was there ever any discussion about this afterwards?"

"Over at the Towne Mall, Jim Antoniotti stated to Bobbi things was taken care of. What he meant by that, I don't know."

"Did anyone ever discuss the murder after that?"

"No."

"Is there anything else you can tell us that you know about the murder?"

"Not offhand. I had the understanding they were going to rough her up and…"

"What do you think happened?"

"That's all I thought was going on. They just roughed her up, because I didn't want involved in no felony rap."

"Okay, Mike, did we threaten you in any way to make this statement?"

"No."

"Did we promise you anything in return for this statement?"

"No."

"Are you willing to testify to what you just told us?"

"Yes."

"Mike, I think that finishes it." After assigning a time, date and location to the tape, the detectives returned to New Castle, convinced they had constructed a solid case.

Atkinson repeated his testimony to Lieutenant Gagliardo and Sergeant Abraham the following morning, including new details. He added the name of Bobby Hall to the plotters who met at the Antoniotti house the night before the murders. Mike also told the police Paul Pounds owned a .22-caliber seven-shot special in addition to his hunting knife.

Lieutenant Piscitelli, Sergeant Abraham and Patrolman Castrucci returned with an arrest warrant for criminal homicide against Mike Atkinson. The police transported the prisoner from the Butler County Jail to District Justice Hanna's office for a formal arraignment and back to his cell again by early afternoon.

8

A SNAG IN THE CASE

Antoniotti and Atkinson's testimony provided both witnesses and a motive. Toward the middle of February, ex-policeman Ralph Williams and Larry Turner, Antoniotti's parole officer, discussed the Kadunce murders. Williams told Turner that the police were housing Antoniotti in the Lawrence County Jail on suspicion of being an accessory to murder.

"Do you think he could be involved in these murders?"

"I don't know. When were the killings?"

"July 11, 1978. Why?"

"You know, I think Antoniotti was in the Western Penitentiary for the Pete's Bait Shop robbery around that time. I'll check my records," Turner answered.

Sure enough, the records confirmed that Antoniotti had been incarcerated on the day of the murders. Obviously, he knew a great deal about the case, but the police had forced a confession from him. The evidence from the state's star witness had just evaporated.

Turner phoned Chief Joe Farris, who blew his stack.

"Gagliardo, what the hell were you thinking? Antoniotti claims you threatened him with a tire iron. You can't pull that crap in this day and age. You've just jeopardized this entire case."

"Chief, he knew his stuff. I thought he was involved. He even knew the layout of the house."

Facts showed Antoniotti had performed odd jobs around the property. In any case, Turner's revelation crushed Gagliardo and Abraham, who freed

Antoniotti, following an apology. Abraham returned to the Butler County Jail to re-interrogate Atkinson.

"Mike, you lied to me. Antoniotti was in Western Penitentiary the day of the Kadunce killings."

"I tried to tell you the husband was involved. You wouldn't hear it."

"Let's start all over again, and no more lies."

Mike Atkinson provided a new statement to Sergeant Abraham on February 12, 1980, at the New Castle detective bureau in the presence of a court-appointed attorney:

> *I met Kathy Kadunce in 1977, around April of that year. It was in the Towne Mall, and Frank Costal introduced us. We talked for a short while, and then the three of us went over to Eat 'n Park and had coffee. I saw Kathy several times after that. I would see her in the mall, and we would just talk. Once or twice she was with Frank Costal. I also saw her at Frank's apartment around four times. All these meetings were in 1977.*
>
> *I met Larry Kadunce at the Towne Mall in the early part of 1978, and he was introduced to me by Kathy Kadunce. She introduced him as her husband. The next time I met Larry Kadunce was in July of 1978, and he was with Frank Costal, John Dudoic, and I think Raymond Thompson. They were in the Burger Chef, and we were talking about some drugs. I gave Frank $105 to get me some speed and Percodan. From there all of us left and went out to the Papermill Bridge near John Dudoic's place to smoke some weed. This was around 11:30 at night. Larry wanted to get some Pepsi, and he left.*
>
> *The next time I saw Larry was on July 10, 1978 in the Burger Chef. John Dudoic and Frank Costal were also there, and it was early in the evening. We were all sitting there, and I asked Frank if he had the drugs that I had paid him for. Frank said that Larry's wife had found them and flushed them down the toilet. I asked Larry, and he said the same thing. I asked him when I could find out for sure, because I wanted to make sure I wasn't being ripped off. Larry told me to ask Kathy, and then he said he had to go. Frank told him that he would see him later.*
>
> *John, Frank and I walked across the street to the car, and Frank asked where we were going, and I told him me and John were going fishing. Frank told us to come by his place after we were done, because he wanted to straighten things out with Kathy. I mentioned she might get roughened up a bit to find out where the drugs were, and Frank told me to do what I wanted. Raymond Thompson came over from the mall, and I asked him if*

he wanted to go fishing, and he started to go with us, but Frank talked him into going up to his place.

John and I then left to go fishing. We were in John's car, and we stopped at the Oasis Bar to get some beer. John was driving an older Gran Prix, and it was a gold color. After we picked up the beer, John and I went fishing at Medusa Lake. We fished til around four, and we were drinking beer and smoking weed. From there, we drove to Frank's place and went up to his apartment and knocked on the door. Frank woke up and answered. When I walked in, I saw Larry in Frank's bed. We had caught some fish, and I asked Frank if he wanted some. Frank said he didn't want the fish, so John and I drove to the Southside to John Dixon's house and gave him the fish. From there we went back to Frank's place.

Frank let us in again, and Larry was still there in bed. Larry was awake, and John and I went into the kitchen and fixed some tea. In a short time Larry came out to the kitchen, and he had on sandals and white cutoff shorts and no shirt. Larry said we should go over and talk to Kathy, cause he had to be at work at a certain time. Larry had a pair of dark overalls with him, and he put them on.

The four of us along with John's white German Shepherd dog went down and got into John's car. Frank and Larry got into the back seat. John was in the right passenger side, while I was driving. I drove onto Wallace to North Jefferson Street. I turned right on North Jefferson to Fast 'n Friendly and pulled in the parking lot from the Wilmington Avenue side.

We all got out of the car and walked behind Fast 'n Friendly. We walked into the first driveway next to the store. Frank and Larry were in front of John and I. John's dog also was with us when we got out of the car. In the driveway, there was a blue car, and up a little further from it was a red car. Frank and Larry went into the house through the back door. John and I followed. We walked up some stairs and into the kitchen. I walked over to the dining room and sat down in a chair. I'm not sure who made the coffee, but it was either Frank or John. Frank handed me a cup of coffee, and I started to drink it. I was sitting near the doorway between the dining room and the front room.

Frank said he had to go to the bathroom, and he went upstairs. I heard the toilet flush. Then, I heard a woman's voice, Larry's voice and Frank's voice, and it sounded like they were arguing over Frank being there, cause I heard Kathy say, "I see you got your God-damn faggot boyfriend with you," and I heard Larry yell, "Well, you have your asshole boyfriend downstairs," and she said "Who?" Larry said, "Mike, and she said,

"*Heavy.*" *There was some more words said, and then Larry came down with a baby bassinette and asked John to help pull the legs out on it.*

I got up and started to walk to the kitchen, and Larry said for me to walk on the plastic runners, cause there was something done to the floor. Larry then went back upstairs, and I could hear water running. John and I were talking downstairs, and I heard a child's voice upstairs say, "Daddy, I have to go to the bathroom," and I heard Larry say, "Get your God-damn ass back in bed," and I heard the child say, "Daddy, I have to go potty," and then I heard Larry say, "Frank, make sure she's in bed, and her ass stays there."

A short time later, Larry called me upstairs to the bathroom. When I walked into the bathroom, Kathy and Larry were still there. I asked both of them what was going on, meaning what happened to my pills, and I turned to Kathy and told her to put a robe on, cause she was standing there in the nude. Larry popped up and said that it would not be the first time that I saw her ass. I sat down on the edge of the tub and asked Kathy what happened to the pills. She said, "What pills?" And Larry popped up and said she did not know anything about the pills.

Larry asked me if I was having an affair with his wife, and he showed me some pictures. I put my cigarette out in the bathtub, and there was hot water in the tub. There was an argument between the three of us about the pictures, and I called Kathy a lying bitch and hit her in the back of the head with an unopened can of beer I had with me. She fell toward Larry, and she looked like she was in a daze. I got up and walked down the stairs.

When I got to the bottom, I heard Kathy and Larry arguing, and she was telling Larry not to pull her hair, and I heard her scream, "Why did you kick me there?"

All the time I was upstairs I did not see Frank, but I could hear him moaning, and it sounded like it came from a room near the bathroom. I heard what sounded like a firecracker come from upstairs. John started to go upstairs, and I followed him. As we were going up, John's dog followed us.

When I got to the top of the stairs, Larry came out of the bathroom, and he was holding a pistol in his hand. I asked him what was going on, and he did not answer me, so I stepped in the bathroom, and I saw Kathy on the bathroom floor with her hands under her, and she was on her knees, and her head was on the floor. She was moaning or crying, and I couldn't understand her. I came back out of the bathroom and grabbed Larry and asked him what was going on, and he started to laugh. Frank came out of a room and stepped between me and John and pushed me aside.

I looked at my shirt, and there was a handprint from blood on my shirt from where Frank pushed me. Frank had something in his right hand, but I don't know what it was. After Frank pushed me, he stepped into the bathroom. I looked at John and told him, "Let's get the hell out of here." We both went down the steps. The dog followed us. Larry already was downstairs.

As we were leaving, I saw Larry taking off his overalls in the dining room. I picked up the ashtray and put it in the sink. John and I went out the back door and over to John's car. We sat there a few minutes, and I asked John what was going on, and he just looked at me and said I was set up.

We pulled out. John was driving on to Wilmington and headed toward town. I was looking back, cause I was scared, and I saw Frank and Larry come out the front of the house. They crossed the street angling toward town. I asked John why Larry was not driving his car, and he told me it was not Larry's car in the driveway. John drove down to the public square, and I told John that our fingerprints were all over the place, and we should go back and clean up.

John turned around going the wrong way in front of the post office. The public square was under construction, and it was blocked to traffic, but there were ramps so we could drive around. We drove back to Larry Kadunce's and parked behind the house. John went inside, and I stayed in the car. When John got out of the car, his dog went to get out, and I grabbed him. As I grabbed, he bit my finger. This was the same finger I had injured before, and I had three stitches put into it.

I sat in the car for about twenty minutes, and John came out with my cigarettes and a lighter, and he gave me hell for leaving them. He also had a knife wrapped in blue jean cloth. John was sick, and he threw up in the car. I drove from there to my house, which is 1010 South Jefferson Street. I pulled in the backyard, and John cleaned the car. I took my shirt and burned it in the backyard. I also burned a plastic runner John had brought out of the house with him, and it had blood all over it.

I went into the house and had some coffee and bandaged my finger. We stayed in my house for around an hour and a half. We left the house and went back to Frank's place. Frank was tripping on acid. John had the knife in his hand, and he asked Frank what he wanted done with the knife. Frank told him to give it to me, and I should get rid of it when I go fishing. John pulled out a couple of rings from his pocket and handed them to Frank and told him to make sure Larry gets them.

We stayed there for a little while, and then me and John drove to Medusa Lake. While we were driving, John handed me six pictures he said he got from underneath Kathy's mattress. I asked John if those were the same pictures Larry showed me, and he told me they weren't. When we got to the lake, I burned the pictures.

From there, we drove to Route 18 and parked the car off the road past the bridge. We got out of the car and walked underneath the bridge and up the side of the hill. We walked back a dirt road leading to a pond. John handed me the knife, and I threw it in the pond. John had thrown a stick in the pond so the dog would chase it and not the knife. We walked back to the car and came back to New Castle. John dropped me off at home and left. On the 12th of July, I left for Mt. Pleasant with my dad.

Although Abraham had Atkinson's new written statement, he intended to check every word for accuracy.

"Chuck, do you know this guy Dudoic? His name rings a bell. We need to question him," Gig said.

"Can't, he killed himself last year. I investigated the case. He looked just like that Beatle John Lennon, and he had a German Shepherd named Schultz. He left a note about not being able to live with himself any longer," Abraham explained. Thirty-three-year-old John Zigmont Dudoic, a Nazi fanatic and worshiper of the occult, shot himself with a .22 on November 19, 1979. Prior to the suicide, he had retired on disability from the New York postal department. A conversation with Dudoic's parents confirmed that Frank Costal had visited him a few hours prior to his death.

"Do you think Costal might have talked him into it?" Gig asked.

"Possibly, but without Dudoic, we've got to place our bets on Atkinson. God help us, but he's the key to the case," Chuck added.

9

TRIAL PREPARATION

S ergeant Charles Abraham, the prosecuting police officer, and his boss Frank Gagliardo, drew up a list of potential witnesses for the upcoming Atkinson-Costal trials. Scores of interviews and the ferreting for evidence forced the two cops to earn their pay. Several interviews provided meaningless, or worse yet, misleading information. Many informants lived in the projects, their statements marred by marginal literacy and limited mental capabilities. Some had served time for burglary or drug abuse.

Gagliardo and Abraham formed a powerful team. Gig, a rough-and-tumble Italian American, tackled crime head on with physical and mental toughness. He didn't like the city's lowlife, and they didn't like him. His hard-boiled "don't lie to me, you son-of-a-bitch" approach combined with a healthy dose of fist thumping to browbeat info and even confessions from many a thug. Off the job, Gig transformed into a model husband and family man who escaped the pressure of his job into the security of a happy home life.

Babe Abraham presented a calmer exterior. He rarely raised his voice, but the easygoing façade masked the internalized stress of police work, his obsession and nemesis. Tension from the job rattled his home life and eventually cost him a divorce.

As a teenager, Chuck earned high grades. After graduation from high school, a sense of direction eluded him. He enlisted in the service and served three years in air defense. He took the admission test for West Point, earning an appointment, but balked at an additional six-year commitment. He

"Babe" Abraham (*left*) and "Gig" Gagliardo. *Courtesy of the New Castle Police Department.*

missed New Castle. After discharge, he drove a truck, worked at a bakery and built boxes for American Cyanamide. Seeking a career, he told his father he intended to take the police examination.

"Why do you want to be a cop? You should go to West Point. You won't meet a good class of people as a cop," his father, a Lebanese immigrant and retired foundry worker, advised. Chuck's father died the Thursday before the test, but Chuck took the exam and passed with a top score.

Abraham's coworkers liked him, especially his knack of listening. Even criminals trusted his coolness and sincerity. Police work had provided the direction he sought.

Gig and Chuck often utilized the classic good cop, bad cop roles. Chuck, a thirty-five-year-old baby-faced teddy bear, who transferred to the detective bureau earlier in the year, played "Mr. Nice Guy." Gig's thinning hair, intensive stare and natural aggressiveness made him the natural attack dog.

Recent politics played a key part in both men's careers. Angelo Sands had just taken office as the mayor of New Castle. Sands's new police chief, Joe Farris, took the opportunity to reward the mayor's supporters. Captain Willie Carbone retired rather than face a demotion. Gig, a one-time police captain and a Sands man, received a promotion to chief of the detective bureau. Farris intended to demote Abraham to beat patrolman since he carried a petition for Sands's losing opponent, Sheriff George Sigler. Gig interceded and got Chuck a spot in the detective bureau.

On February 12, 1981, Chuck and Gig parlayed in the city building basement to map out an interview strategy. As Chuck sucked in the smoke from his Kent, Gig polished off his coffee. They opted to visit the Bowers home on Halco Drive in the projects, a place Costal had frequented.

The cops knocked on the door, and a middle-aged man answered.

"Mr. Bowers?"

"Yes?"

"We are from the New Castle police, and we would like to talk to your boys about an investigation we are working on."

Mr. Bowers opened the door and offered coffee to the officers. They passed. Mr. Bowers asked his sons, nineteen-year-old Wesley and twelve-year-old Patrick, to come into the living room. Wesley communicated with difficulty. He slurred his words, periodically glancing toward his brother, who helped him finish sentences. He remembered visiting Costal's apartment, where Frank had given him grass to smoke and asked him to rip off some local merchants.

"Sometimes, Frank walked up Canyon Avenue past Fast 'n Friendly on Wilmington on his way home," Wesley continued. "Once, a lady called him a witch. The two got into a real shouting match, and Costal left in a huff after placing a curse on her." The youth talked about buying a .22 rifle from Frank for five dollars. His father sold the gun to the Greek owner of the Black Whale. Wesley told the police that Costal once accused him of killing a woman and child. Abraham wondered if Costal intended to brainwash the slow-witted boy into implicating himself in the Kadunce killings.

The detectives checked out Wesley's rifle story with the owner of the Black Whale, a sleazy bar in an alley off Washington Street in downtown. The proprietor confirmed the purchase, explaining that he resold the weapon to a man who lived on Englewood. Following up the lead, the police asked the owner to examine the gun. The serial number revealed it had been registered to Henry Rowe, a one-time roommate of Costal's, who moved to New York in May 1978. A record check of the gun proved negative. Wesley's gun story produced minimal intel—a dead end.

The police next questioned Steve Hammond, a teenage friend of the Bowers boys, who believed, "Frank had the power of the devil. He could make anybody do things." Hammond thought Costal knew his every move. Costal had plied him with marijuana and committed homosexual acts with him. Hammond had trouble voicing his story, and Abraham listened, sympathizing with the boy's mental deficiency and fear of the devil man.

"Chuck, do you think Costal really could be a witch?" Gig asked, half in jest.

"Isn't a male witch called a warlock?" Chuck answered.

"Beats me, but doesn't Costal think he might be half woman?" Both laughed, releasing the tension of the investigation for a minute.

Marshall Dillon, an uncooperative teenager, became another target for questioning. Gig dragged him to the station to loosen his tongue. After some pressure, Dillon admitted to rooming with Costal. He refused to provide additional particulars.

"My gut tells me he knows more. We have to question him again later," Gig told Chuck.

That same day, a woman named Jane Garcia called the station. She offered information about Frank Costal. Lastoria, Abraham and Gagliardo hopped into an unmarked white Plymouth and headed to the Garcia home, where an attractive five-foot-two bleached blond in her late forties greeted them. Jane and Frank had been friends.

When Costal entered the hospital for chest pains in late 1978, Jane took care of his apartment and fed his pet parrot. When she visited his hospital room, she claimed she had seen a visitor who resembled Lou Kadunce.

Following Costal's release from the hospital, Jane and her daughter drove to Frank's apartment to return his key. Costal answered the door wearing red underwear and nylon hose. He introduced Jane to his "girlfriend, a man named 'Lori,'" clad in a tee shirt and blue jeans. She believed Lori was the same person she had seen at the hospital.

The cops made a note to check the Jameson Hospital records to confirm the veracity of the story, since Costal and Kadunce denied knowing each other. Garcia's interview contradicted their stories.

Jane spoke about Costal's cult and how he controlled his followers with sex, drugs, liquor and threats. She mentioned the name of Tom Reese and said he might know something.

Reese, a man in his late twenties, thought Costal and Speed Reuter might have been involved in the drowning of Tyrone Hambrick. Reese knew Kathy and Lou Kadunce but couldn't be sure if they knew Costal. Frank talked to him about blood sacrifices and Mary Black, the legendary witch buried in Turkey Hill, but he refused to reveal the rituals of his cult to Reese, an outsider, who had declined to join his cult. He remembered Costal owning a silvery .22- or .32-caliber pistol.

Prior to lunch, Jane Garcia came to the detective bureau for additional questioning. When Abraham showed her a photograph of Larry Kadunce, she identified him as Lori. She also mentioned that Frank bragged he could get rid of her husband for twenty-five dollars if he ever mistreated her.

Myrna Miller, an acquaintance of Tom Reese's, appeared at the station with a story from a friend named Dave McClaren. He claimed "Frank Costal had done it, and no one would ever know the reason why." When the police visited McClaren at his house, he backed down from the account he had told Myrna, swearing, "It was just the alcohol talking." The team left, convinced he really knew nothing.

Costal's niece Marge Baker, a heavyset woman with a house full of kids, reacted to an interruption of her day with silence. Gig jarred a response from her: "Why don't you get me a cup of coffee?"

Baker snapped, "I'm not your slave."

"Relax, we just want to talk. Just give us a little information," Gig said. Baker opened up and provided a handful of names. Her uncle hung out with Mike Atkinson and Paul Pounds. She had lived with Pounds, and Mike pointed a gun at her in June 1978 after she refused to go out with him. Gig thanked her for the information and left.

Darlene Pounds Miller, the gangly thirty-two-year-old divorced sister of Paul Pounds, dated Mike in May 1978. She and Mike lived together for several weeks until they broke up on July 6. She confirmed that Mike belonged to Frank's cult and owned a pistol.

Interviewee Sheryl Tanner disclosed that her husband, Raymond, ran around with Costal and Atkinson most of 1975, prior to his incarceration at Huntingdon State Penitentiary for kidnaping and terroristic threats against a minor. Abraham felt sympathy for this chunky woman who had married the wrong guy.

"Did Mike Atkinson have a gun?"

"Yes, he had a pistol."

She mentioned Costal's prophecy that her husband would die from a gun.

"Did you ever hear anything about Costal or Atkinson being involved in a killing?" Abraham asked. She heard a rumor Atkinson had killed someone. She believed guilt caused John Dudoic to kill himself, just as it had to her own husband.

Sheryl Tanner called the detective bureau later in the day to fill in some details. She recalled her husband returning home one evening in November 1975 and slogging to the basement. Red splotches smeared Raymond's clothing. When his wife asked what happened, he ignored her question. He slipped off his shirt and destroyed it. Following that night, he "began to act funny."

Both Chuck and Gig assumed Raymond Tanner had played a role in the unsolved murders of four-year-old Melanie Gargasz and her thirty-seven-year-old babysitter Beverly Withers on November 6, 1975, on Old Pulaski Road. Guilt probably led to his suicide. Could Atkinson and Costal have been involved as well?

Jane Garcia brought two books to the detective bureau that she borrowed from Frank Costal: *The Witches Bible* with the name "Frank Batzel" written on the inside cover and "Larry K." beneath and *Drum and Candle* with "L Kadunce" on the inside cover and "Frank" on the facing page.

Frank boasted to Jane that "he had the power to separate from his body any cult member who failed to obey his orders." Just prior to the summer of 1978, John Dudoic, Mike Atkinson and a man named Bill appeared at her house. Costal had ordered them to be ready to take someone out of his body, but they did not know which of them would be chosen for the task or exactly what the act might be. They did not want to do whatever it was and asked how to get out of it. Jane could not provide an answer.

Each interview added names to the list of those who needed to be questioned. Jane Garcia's daughter Susan came to the bureau at her mother's request. Abraham empathized with the comely lady with a pronounced limp from a stroke. She visited Costal's apartment in 1978. When she asked why he had plastic bats on his lampshades, he explained that each one represented a member of his cult.

Costal claimed he could cure her limp if she removed her clothes and got into the bathtub. Susan refused.

"Can you think of anything else?" Abraham asked.

"Yes, he talked about Tyrone Hambrick's drowning, but I can't remember exactly what he said."

An interview with John Dudoic's parents followed. Mrs. Dudoic, a short, matronly lady, babbled incessantly. Abraham nicknamed her "motormouth." Her husband remained less talkative.

Abraham thought back after meeting Mr. and Mrs. Dudoic on the day of John's suicide. He had been the first cop on the scene, inspecting the body and spotting the .22 pistol in his hand. A suicide note sat perched on a typewriter. He willed his stereo to friends and his Nazi flag to a guy named Bob in Portersville. He closed the note with "advertise for a good home for Schultz." John's father told the police that "his son had not been right since that Pagley thing," referring to the disappearance of one of his son's acquaintances who never resurfaced.

During the current interrogation, the Dudoics spoke of their son burning a stack of papers in the furnace the day of his death. Abraham asked for permission to examine John's effects. As he walked toward the bedroom, John's dog Schultz, named for the German guard on the television show *Hogan's Heroes*, moped on the living room floor with his head buried beside his paws. The dog raised his head and sniffed at Abraham. Smelling nothing to set off his protective instincts, the dog lowered his dark-brown eyes and returned to his solitude. The search uncovered several satanic books, including *The Black Arts* and *The Satanic Bible*. The parents provided little else.

Elaine Callahan, a name mentioned by Mrs. Dudoic as a friend of her son, told the police John had visited her apartment a few days before his suicide. He handed her several poems on death and dying. As his voice trembled, she asked what was wrong.

"It's all wrong," he stammered, battling to release some buried pain. "I can't take it much longer." She asked if he wanted to tell her anything. "I don't want to say anything," he continued. Elaine believed John could have provided the key to the Kadunce case had he lived.

Elaine revealed several interesting incidents concerning Frank. "He asked me to join his cult as a high priestess, but I declined." When John and Frank spent time together in her presence, they whispered like a couple of teenage girls, excluding her. "Frank became jealous if any of his boyfriends spoke to a woman in his presence." Costal confided that he and Mike had been "lovers." Elaine discussed a seance where Frank warned Sheryl Tanner that her husband would die from a gun.

John Dudoic. *Courtesy of the New Castle Police Department.*

Just days after John's death, Elaine met Costal at Burger Chef for a coffee. Frank told her he had spent four hours with John the day of the suicide. She noticed Frank appeared unfazed by the death of his so-called best friend.

While Abraham and Gagliardo continued their pursuit of Atkinson for the Kadunce murders, other actions reached the courts. District Magistrate Wayne Shaffer ordered Atkinson's father bound over to the grand jury for hindering his son's apprehension on the rape charge. That same day, Judge Glenn McCracken denied a motion made by Mike Atkinson's attorney, George Micacchione, to dismiss the rape charge due to the violation of the 180-day rule, which guarantees a speedy trial to the accused.

The rape trial proceeded in short order. Mike Atkinson testified that he and his son went fishing at Medusa Lake on September 5, 1978, along with some friends. Everyone had been drinking. He claimed Ronald Thompson's sixteen-year-old date tried to buy marijuana from him. "When I refused, she threatened to get even with me." As Atkinson fudged through his statement, compounding one contradiction after another, his story lacked believability.

Slow, plodding Raymond Thompson, Ronald's brother, who previously received a three-to-eight-year sentence for his part in the rape, testified that Mike, Ronald, the girl and he had parked by a store in Wampum. Ronald wanted some cigarettes and got out of the car. As soon as Ronald entered the store, Atkinson drove away to a secluded spot, where he held a knife to the girl's throat, raping her and forcing Raymond to take part afterward.

Following five days of testimony, the jury found Atkinson guilty, remanding him to the Lawrence County Jail until sentencing.

Even while the rape trial was in progress, Gig and Chuck continued their interviews. On February 27, the police called Robert Brightshue, a former lover of Costal's who lived in Florida. He spoke with a tough-guy mouth.

"Bobbie, we suggest you think carefully about your attitude and get back to us with some answers," Chuck calmly but forcefully suggested.

That evening, Brightshue called. He admitted to having an affair with Costal, who nicknamed him "Bobbie." Frank had Bobbie call him "Francine." Costal's diary confirmed the intensity of their relationship.

After prodding, Brightshue discussed Costal's cult. He watched him curse an enemy by forcing the blade of a knife through a plastic skull, claiming his intended victim would die. "Tom Reese, Brenda Withers, the Antoniottis, Terry and Jerry Silvis and Mary Akers all hung around the apartment," Brightshue offered.

"Did you know a man called Lori, mid-sized with glasses?" Abraham asked. Brightshue wasn't sure, but recalled a man about five-foot-ten with a medium build, light hair and a thin mustache.

Robert had been married to a woman named Carol Rosfield at that time. Costal was extremely jealous of her or any other women who even spoke to him. At the time of his interview, Brightshue was living with Linda Altman, a niece of Beverly Withers, the babysitter who had been murdered in 1975. This coincidence gave the detectives more questions on which to chew. The Gargasz-Withers murders had never been solved, and Brightshue, and possibly Atkinson and Costal, knew the niece and daughter of the murdered Beverly Withers. Brightshue also stated Costal was acquainted with Kadunce's one-time girlfriend, Mary Akers, as well as his nephews, the Silvises.

"We are going to get the husband," Chuck said.

"Yea, but the DA and Chief Ferris want us to concentrate on Costal and Atkinson for now," Gig answered.

A few days later, the detectives spoke to Brightshue again. They asked how many times Terry and Jerry Silvis had visited Costal's apartment. He couldn't say.

"How's about Mary Akers?" He recalled seeing her five or six times. Occasionally, a man came with her, but Brightshue couldn't describe him.

The next day, Chuck and Gig called in Lisa Akers, Mary's sister. She had visited the apartment with three friends but felt too frightened to enter. On another occasion, she and some friends met Frank at the grave of Mary

Black, a reputed witch who died in 1888. Costal, dressed in his high priest's robe, told his audience that Mary Black's spirit had transmigrated to a giant black cat with green eyes that could stare right through you.

"Lisa, did you know Larry Kadunce?" Abraham asked.

"Yes, through my sister. I thought he was very nice."

Mary Akers told the police she knew Costal only by sight but had never entered his apartment. It was possible Brightshue had confused Mary with her sister.

Chuck drove to Dee's restaurant at Bailey's Truck Stop on Route 422 East for lunch, a frequent stop for him. His mother-in-law owned the place, and he co-signed some notes at the bank for her. He parked himself at the counter, and the waitress poured a cup of coffee for him without asking. He ordered a steak sandwich.

Chuck reached across the counter for the cream. Pouring a healthy slurp, he watched it swirl around the cup in a cotton-colored cloud, reminding him of the haze of unhappiness roiling through his personal life. The Kadunce case had consumed him, robbing his family of his attention and time. He sipped the coffee and sighed, determined to change his lifestyle once this wretched case ended.

Glancing to his right, he recognized Ted Brown, a loser who had been in and out of trouble due to drugs much of his adult life. Brown, caught up in his own reverie, toyed with his own coffee. He reached into his shirt pocket for a smoke. When he pulled out the pack, a small bag of grass plopped on the counter. Abraham reached over and snatched the package before Brown's eyes.

"What's this, Ted?" The color drained from the other man's face.

"You ain't gonna bust me for that, are you?"

Abraham had his hands full. Brown really wasn't too bad a soul. Besides, the courts would probably let him off with a slap on the wrist for such a small quantity of grass.

"Tell you what, I'm going to let it slide this time." Abraham walked around the counter and flushed the grass down the sink. "But you have to keep clean."

"Yea, I owe you one," Ted eagerly answered, thrilled to be off the hook.

Within the week, Abraham's generosity paid dividends. Brown called him at the station.

"You still working on the Kadunce case?"

"Yes, Ted."

"I suggest you go see Stacy Reed. She used to live on Canyon. She may know something."

Abraham thanked Brown and hung up the phone. Poor Ted, a reliable informant, later ran into more problems with the law, ending up in Western Penitentiary, where he hanged himself in a fit of depression. Babe tacked the name Stacy Reed to his interview list.

The detectives first called on Ruby Angry, a street-smart, heavyset African American woman from Neshannock Village. Mike Atkinson provided her name. When she tossed out some backtalk, Gig threatened to drag her to the station. She chose to cooperate, offering the fact that Mike stayed at her home in 1977. She remembered him having a gun.

"Did you ever see it?" Gig asked.

"Sure did."

"What did it look like?" Ruby described a pistol with white handles. The police found a fragment from a white pistol handle at the Gargasz-Withers murder scene.

"Do you remember if the handle was broken or chipped?" Chuck asked. Ruby didn't know.

Ruby added a parting shot. She once washed one of Mike's T-shirts with what looked like a bloodstain. She could not remember the month or even the year.

Ron Thompson contacted the station. The police had picked him up on a drunk-and-disorderly charge, and he wanted to trade leniency for some info. His brother Raymond, an inmate at the Lawrence County Jail who was testifying at the Atkinson rape trial, claimed to have spoken to Costal about the Kadunce case.

The detectives picked up Ron at his second-floor walkup near the central fire station to check out his story. Chuck commented on the plaster cast on his arm.

"Broke it in a fight with my girlfriend. I jumped off the viaduct and got messed up."

"Okay, what can you give us on the Kadunce case?" Gig demanded, cutting off the chitchat.

"You know my brother and Frank Costal are locked in the can together. Well, Frank told Ray that he and Mike were at the Kadunce house when the murder took place, but he stayed in the car. Costal claimed Mike returned to the car with blood all over him."

"How do we know we can believe you?" Gig asked. Ron allowed the detectives to tape his statement and offered to accompany them to the Lawrence County Jail to talk to his slow-witted brother, temporarily transferred from Rockview Penitentiary to testify at the rape trial. They sat in the tiny holding cell and began the interrogation. Abraham had an aversion to tight places, and the inmate's plodding speech made the interview long and uncomfortable. Raymond Thompson's voice displayed his fear of the high priest.

"Go on, Raymond, he can't hurt you now," Ronald urged, placing his hand on his brother's shoulder for encouragement.

"He said they were in Mike's blue Mustang, and they drove up to that lady's house, and he stayed in the car. I didn't ask him nothing else."

"Who were you talking to?" Raymond clammed up.

"Weren't you talking to Frank Batzel?" Ron asked his brother.

"Yes, I was talking to Frank Bat…er…um," Raymond stammered.

"Was he also called Costal?" Chuck asked.

"Yes, I think his real name is Costal, but I know him as the high priest…"

"Did he talk about the Kadunce thing?"

"Yes, he said Mike Atkinson was the one who went inside the house, and when he came out, he had blood all over him. He told me that…" Raymond stared blankly into space.

"What did he tell you?" Abraham prodded.

"That he was at Burger Chef that morning, and Mike picked him up and told him he had to go somewhere. I don't want to say no more." Raymond covered his mouth with his right hand.

The interview ended shortly before lunch after twenty interminable minutes.

"That was like pulling teeth," Chuck complained to Gig out of Ronald's hearing.

"This Raymond is more than one brick short of a load." Gig agreed. Ronald Thompson's problems compounded over the next year. He jumped to his death while stoned on drugs in 1982.

Later in the day, Gig and Chuck paid a call on Stacy Reed, a lady in her mid-twenties and one of the few credible leads, whose name had been suggested by Ted Brown. Stacy lived on Canyon, a few blocks from the Kadunce house. On the morning of the murders, she awakened at 6:30 a.m., intending to visit her husband at the Gateway Rehabilitation Center, where he had been undergoing treatment. She opened the dining room drapes facing the hill leading to Wilmington to check out the weather and spotted two men walking down the roadway. One looked tall and had brown hair. The other wore his hair long and had a beard. When a black man in a beige car approached, the pair scooted off the road and disappeared into the woods. Stacy thought their behavior strange but went about her plans.

Returning from Gateway, she spotted the ambulance parked near Fast 'n Friendly. She gave the matter little thought until her mother told her about the Kadunce murders.

"How come you waited so long to talk about this? Why didn't you call that day?" Abraham asked.

"I did. I telephoned the police station to report the incident the evening of the murders, but no one called me back." Abraham made a note to check out the station's call records.

Stacy Reed continued. A friend, Randy Perrota, took her to visit Frank Costal at his apartment a few months later. She recognized him as one of the two men she saw the day of the murders. She visited the apartment on three other occasions, and each time Costal spoke about his cult.

The interview ended with Stacy pointing to the spot where the two men had disappeared into the woods.

Stacy Reed's view off Canyon. *Author's collection.*

As Chuck left the Reed house, he said, "Gig, I believe her. She had perfect visibility from her back window. I think we have an eyewitness. I'm going to check out her story about calling the station." Sure enough, Chuck discovered a note made by Leon Sasiadek on July 11, 1978. Sas reported it to Chief Carbone, but the police were so convinced of the husband's guilt, they ignored the lead.

Abraham received permission to photograph the interior of the Highland Avenue apartment from Costal's sister. Chuck's religious upbringing and claustrophobia complicated the assignment. He loaded the department's 35-millimeter camera with film and snapped forty shots. Each click of the shutter felt like some supernatural power snatching at his soul. The blood-red candles, the plastic bats, the altar with a skull and the satanic pictures on the walls shook his composure. He imagined curses flowing through Costal's thick lips as he hurried to complete his task.

A few days later, Chuck realized he had failed to thread the film when the roll came back blank. After checking out the pictures taken the day of Costal's arrest, the detectives determined additional pictures would be unnecessary.

The web of guilt spun by the motley cast of interviewees convinced the police of the strength of their case. The motive and evidence proved fairly solid. Costal's homosexuality, carny background, demonic appearance and devil worship combined with Atkinson's penchant for violence strengthened the odds of a conviction. Still, the detectives continued their interviews.

Paul Pounds, the brother of Darlene Pounds Miller, put on a show of machismo. Gig was having none of it.

"Pounds, don't give us any crap or we'll haul you right to the station. All we want is a few answers, and you can go on your way. Your choice."

Pounds changed his attitude.

"I didn't like Atkinson much," Pounds offered. He had argued with him after his sister and Mike had broken up the week before the Kadunce killings. Pounds said that Mike tried to implicate him in the murders "to get even." Atkinson had told Pounds he owned a .22 pistol, but he never had seen it.

Pounds met Costal through Marge Baker, Frank's niece. He only visited Costal's apartment one time but left after five minutes. "I didn't go for that voodoo stuff."

Pounds denied any knowledge of the crime and volunteered to take a lie detector to prove his innocence. Gig considered Pounds a punk, but he believed him.

The police next tracked down Costal's twenty-eight-year-old niece, Kathy Laux, hauling her to the station for questioning. Atkinson's original statement claimed Kathy Kadunce had ripped him off for some windowpane acid. Subsequently, Atkinson changed his story, claiming he had confused Kathy Kadunce with Kathy Laux.

"What can you tell us about Mike Atkinson?" asked Gig.

"I have known Mike for around six years. I never went out with him, and I never had sex with him. He got mad at me, because I wouldn't go out with him. He said he was going to get in my pants sooner or later."

Kathy denied any involvement in a drug deal with Atkinson or her uncle, and claimed, as far as she knew, she was Frank's favorite niece.

On March 13, Atkinson's court-appointed attorney, George Micacchione, requested a continuance of the Kadunce trial. With the rape trial recently completed and the Puz investigation still underway, the attorney requested additional time to prepare his defense. The judge rescheduled the hearing for early April.

Atkinson had babbled during a prior interview about Costal asking him to get rid of a damaged .22-caliber pistol. Mike claimed he sold it to a black man named Williams. On March 15, Gig and Chuck drove to the rundown Crescentdale apartment of Andrew "Slim" Williams on the outskirts of Wampum to ask about the gun. Slim remembered Atkinson seeing him in June or July 1978. "He pulled out a .22-caliber, nickel-plated revolver from his pocket and said, 'I'm short on cash. I want fifteen dollars for it.'"

Slim asked to see it. He pointed to a crack on the cylinder. "I ain't payin' you fifteen dollars for no broken gun."

"What would you give?" Atkinson countered.

Williams counted out the cash in his pocket. "All I got is $1.28 and an old radio."

"Okay, you've got a deal." Mike handed over the gun and left. When Slim checked the gun carefully, the crack looked worse than he thought. Recognizing the pistol would be dangerous to use, he threw it in the woods behind his house. Later, he burned the holster that went with it.

"Bingo, I think we've got ourselves a murder weapon," Gig announced. The detectives ordered a metal detector, but an extensive search failed to uncover the missing gun.

As the date for his trial neared, Atkinson tossed out an alibi, claiming to have been in Mount Pleasant with Darlene Pounds to visit his sister on the day of the murder. Abraham re-interviewed Darlene to verify Mike's story.

Darlene stated she had traveled to Mount Pleasant with Atkinson in early June, not July. She explained that she was positive about the month. "I'm sure, because I had to make a special trip back to New Castle on June 7 for a child support hearing." She attended the hearing and returned to Mount Pleasant in her green station wagon for approximately a week.

"I spent July 4 at my home, not Mount Pleasant," Darlene continued. She claimed she had broken up with Mike prior to the holiday and he left her house in an uproar, moving in with his father. She added that Mike could not have driven to Mount Pleasant in her vehicle since it stopped running a few days before the fourth. She parked the station wagon behind her apartment and never drove it again. A few weeks later, she sold it to Jim Johnson through Community Auto Sales. The records confirmed she had transferred the auto on July 17, 1978. Mike's alibi leaked lies.

The police picked up twenty-four-year-old Thomas Shaffer as a suspect in a shoe store burglary. Sergeant Lastoria noted he served time in the Lawrence County Jail from November 12, 1979, through March 12, 1980. Standard procedure encouraged the questioning of detainees regarding their knowledge of other crimes.

"Hey, Shaffer, did you know a guy named Costal while you were in the can?" Lastoria asked.

"Sure did," Shaffer answered. "We were in the same cell block." Lastoria called in Gig and Chuck. Shaffer, a lanky felon with a scruffy look, considered robbery his God-given right, and he seemed good at it. He opened up without prodding:

Sometime in February of '80, me, Richard Garr, George Greer, Frank Costal and George Robinson were sitting in the north section of the jail. We started talking about what we was in there for. Frank Costal bragged how he killed a lady and her daughter. He talked about how he and his friend went into some house next to a store. He said the woman had messed him up, and he wanted revenge. He talked about how they went upstairs, and the woman started to scream. He said he stabbed the woman and carved her up with a big knife. He talked about how the blood was on the wall and on the floor. He then talked about stabbing the little girl and carving her up because he didn't want to be identified. All the time he was describing this, he got excited and high strung, especially when he discussed the blood on the walls and floor. To me it seemed like he enjoyed what he had done. To make friends with us, Frank Costal would give us blowjobs and buy us cigarettes and candy from the commissary. One time he asked me to pass a note to Mike Atkinson, and I did. I don't know what was in the note.

Frank urged Shaffer to join his cult. "He jabbered about power, rituals and witchcraft, sometimes chanting in a weird language." Costal claimed he could get even with his enemies by sticking pins in a doll representing their bodies.

Shaffer also disclosed that Atkinson's father had offered him $1,000 not to testify against Mike. The detectives thought Shaffer would make a great witness if he was for real.

Officer Smith grabbed Gig and Chuck. He recalled driving north on Highland on a Sunday evening in September 1978. "I observed Lou Kadunce and a white female getting out of his vehicle, which was parked facing north on the 1200 block of Highland." Smith could not remember which house he entered. Smith made a report, but the sketchy account proved inadmissible for court use.

Lou Kadunce's nephew Ron "Bud" Silvis claimed he had seen Costal at the Towne Mall but never spoke to him. He had traded books on witchcraft with Kathy Kadunce. He gave the detectives copies of books belonging to Lou Kadunce, including *The Omen*, with the initials "RB" and "FB" printed on the back cover, and *Dracula*, which had the name "Frank" printed on the first page.

"Gig, do you suppose FB stands for Frank Batzel?"

"I wonder if RB might be Bobbie Brightshue?" Chuck guessed.

When the detectives showed a photo of Mike Atkinson to Stacy Reed, she stared at it for several seconds. "He looks a lot like one of the men, but the guy I saw had much longer hair." Mike wore his hair longer in 1978.

Stacy's friend Randy Perrotta claimed he met Costal in 1974. He liked to take girls to his apartment to check out their reaction. On one afternoon, Mike and Frank asked him to take an item to the basement of a house near the courthouse. The guys refused to tell him what he carried, but Mike worried the police were watching him. Perrotta refused, and Mike dropped the subject.

"Costal always talked about the cult and was putting curses on people he didn't like." Once he cursed Henry Rowe, but Perrotta never found out if anything happened.

The detectives rousted twenty-one-year-old James Zingaro, a name provided by Steve Hammond. Zingaro's niece Carol Montgomery accompanied him to the station.

A timid Zingaro told his story: "It was May or June of 1978. I was at Costal's apartment. Steve Hammond and Marshall Dillon were there too. Frank started to talk about a Kathy and her husband. He said he wished her husband would leave her. I asked Costal what he meant. Costal told me she was some chick who lived on Wilmington near Mooney's dump. As he spoke, he grew angry, and his eyes got big."

The day after the murders, Zingaro sat in a booth with Dillon and Costal at Burger Chef. Zingaro asked if Frank heard about the killings on Wilmington. Costal started laughing "real loud." He made a face and said, "That was too bad, but it didn't mean anything to him." After that, he never discussed Kathy or her husband again.

On March 31, Atkinson appeared before District Justice Wayne Shaffer on charges of burglary, receiving of stolen property, murder and arson for the Rosie Puz case. Shaffer set a date of April 8 for the proceeding. An armed guard returned the handcuffed prisoner to the Lawrence County Jail without bail.

The morning of April 1, District Magistrate Howard Hanna initiated formal hearings on the Kadunce case. Attorney George Micacchione represented Atkinson, and Robert Barletta and Harry Falls spoke for Costal. Barletta, a Notre Dame graduate, presented cogent reasoning, while Micacchione, a natural showman, demonstrated great passion and a thorough understanding of the law.

District Attorney Don Williams argued that "the state had built a strong and credible case against the defendants." Atkinson's earlier testimony placed both Costal and Atkinson at the scene of the crime on the day of the murders. Following several days of testimony, Hanna ordered Costal and Atkinson bound over for grand jury action on April 9.

The day of the hearing, a guard discovered Costal in the medical cell with his wrists slashed. He wound towels around the cuts to slow the bleeding and rushed him to St. Francis Hospital for treatment. The injuries proved superficial, and the guard, upset about having to file a fistful of reports, unceremoniously returned the prisoner to jail.

Costal explained his action to the authorities: "They had put me in the medical room after I complained of chest pains and nausea. I've had heart problems before, and my nerves were bad. They had me in a hospital cell, but I called it a detention cell. All I had was a lousy cot and a urinal. The room was a filthy hole and real dirty. I didn't want to kill myself. I took this screw from the wall and cut myself. I didn't want to do myself in. I just wanted out of that little room."

Before cutting himself, Costal had jotted his thoughts on a piece of paper: "To be given to my lawyer in court: I think I committed some murders. I don't know how they were done. I may have dreamed or heard voices that said I did some things. I think I'm crazy. I talk to myself and the TV, too.... My mind will be okay, I'm sure. I need some rest and a clear mind." He set the pencil down and recollected his thoughts. The bareness of the cell strangled his ability to think clearly. He picked up the pencil and wrote: "I did not commit any crimes except bad checks. As for the murders, I only know what was told to me by my lawyer at Justice Hanna's office the day of the hearing. I pleaded not guilty in court. I still hear voices, and the sounds I hear are confusing, but I only hope they will go away. I am in a very nervous state of mind and need psychiatric help. I was under care at Human Services until I came here." Caught up in a haze of conflicting sensations, Costal signed his name to the paper and stared at his words. Dreams of escape into his special world of mysticism and the miraculous Frankie-Francine floated through his mind.

During April, a handful of Lawrence County Jail prisoners conducted a mock trial accusing Atkinson of murdering Dawn Kadunce. Although the inmates would allow robbery and even the murder of an adult to slide, they refused to stomach butchery of a child. Mike's fellow inmates intended to humble him. Prisoner Robert Grim opened a jailhouse tribunal by pointing his finger at Atkinson's face and accusing him of slicing up the child. Atkinson averted his gaze and denied any involvement.

"Look at me when I speak," Grim demanded. "You're a squealer and a baby killer. Now you're going to pay." Rumor of Mike ratting on a prisoner named Alexander, accused of murder, floated throughout the jail.

"I didn't turn no one in, and I didn't kill no baby. I didn't do that part. Frank did it," Atkinson protested.

Derek Fuqua, a muscled African American, seized Atkinson by the shirt and tossed him to the ground. "You killed that child, admit it."

"I didn't do no child." Atkinson glared at his accusers to project toughness, but sweat dripped down his cheeks.

"Listen, mother, you gotta pay." Grim announced. "I am your judge and executioner." Grim signaled Fuqua, who kicked the fallen Atkinson in the ribs.

Other prisoners demanded punishment, believing Atkinson to be an informant. When they pounced on him, Atkinson screamed to draw the guards, who broke up the pummeling.

"Get me out of here. They're going to kill me," Atkinson pleaded.

"Atkinson, you're a pain in the ass, but we'll take you to isolation."

Mike proved a demanding and difficult inmate. Warden Joseph Gregg transferred him to the Beaver County Jail without conducting a formal investigation of the incident. Mike became a problem prisoner in his new setting as well. He alerted the warden of an impending prison break. An investigation revealed that Mike had instigated the proposed escape.

In early May, Judge William Balph set a hearing date for District Attorney Williams to show why Atkinson and Costal should not be released due to false eyewitness statements. The defense argued that Atkinson was arrested on an invalid warrant that failed to meet the Pennsylvania Rules of Criminal Procedure since the police based the affidavit of probable cause on false information provided by James Antoniotti. The judge agreed to rule on the matter shortly.

Atkinson appeared before District Magistrate Shaffer regarding the Puz murder case. Shaffer denied a motion by Attorney Micacchione to dismiss the burglary and receiving of stolen property charges.

The formal hearing included testimony from Fire Chief Brest, Lawrence County deputy coroner P.O. Contrucci and two state police officers. Neighbor Hilda Balmini recalled seeing the station wagon owned by John Atkinson, the defendant's father, parked in front of the Puz apartment at 5:45 p.m. on January 16, the evening of the fire. Tom Hall testified about Mike's bloodstained shirt and his discussion with the defendant about how long a lighted candle would take to ignite a room with a gas stove and open jets. William Puz, the deceased's son, identified several items taken from the Hall house that belonged to his mother. He recognized a copper tub kept in his mother's basement. Julius Miskoicze, owner of Jul's Auto Repairs, testified to purchasing the tub from Atkinson for fifteen dollars.

While the Puz hearing continued, Gagliardo and Abraham proceeded with their own preparation for the Kadunce trial. Respondent Andrea Montgomery described Costal's attempt to lure her into his cult with promises of power. At Judy's house, Frank bragged about beating and stabbing someone named Paul, who turned out to be ex-roommate Paul Weiblinger. Andrea added the name Tom Reese back in the mix: "I bet he knows plenty."

"Like what?" Gig chimed in to open the subject.

"He said the little Kadunce boy wasn't killed because Larry Kadunce made Frank promise he would not hurt the boy. Frank was just to roughen Kathy up." She stated she met Atkinson in 1976. "He asked me to go out with him, but I never did. I thought he was a little crazy or something....Can I go now?" Once Montgomery received the okay to leave, she scampered out of the detective bureau.

In mid-May, after researching the issue, Judge Balph ruled that the arrests of Costal and Atkinson were valid, regardless of the legitimacy of the affidavit of probable cause, bringing the trial a step closer.

Paul Weiblinger, now an inmate in the Allegheny Jail for burglary, became the next targeted interview for the detectives. Weiblinger, a twenty-nine-year-old, nondescript, midsized felon, hung around with Costal in 1977. He confirmed Andrea's story about Costal's temper tantrum, having to wrestle him to the ground and disarm him of a sword. Paul recalled Costal telling him, "Satan was everything. Praised be his name. I am the high priest." Weiblinger believed Costal possessed powers.

"Did he get violent with you?" Gig asked.

"Violent, you'd better believe it." Weiblinger threw out a time when Costal and his brother-in-law beat him for taking something from the apartment. One man shoved him onto the couch and stabbed at his leg with a sword. They dragged him down the stairs to a camper truck and to another house, where the brother-in-law threatened to cut off his balls. After tossing him against the wall, they loaded him back in the vehicle and drove toward Judy Antoniotti's. Along the way, his captors talked of killing him and tossing his body into the quarry. "I was scared and kept quiet." When the camper reached Judy's, the two men laughed and released him.

"Paul, if we could spring you from the joint for a day, would you come to New Castle to make a statement?" Chuck asked.

"Hey, you get me out of here for a day, and you've got a deal."

After receiving the necessary court order, Weiblinger found himself in New Castle. Abraham wanted to know what made Costal tick. He figured out Atkinson, a bully and a coward, a human production gone awry, a classic psychopath and a killing machine, a lowlife who preyed on women and children. Mike took what he wanted when he wanted it without consideration for his victims. He lacked a soul.

Costal appeared more difficult to decipher. He played many roles. While a powerful high priest to his coterie of misfits, he morphed into an unassuming suck-up for the police. Abraham had never encountered such a strange and fascinating adversary.

Weiblinger's story provided an example of Costal's fiery temper. "He went crazy when he caught me playing cards with this girl across the hall from his apartment. He screamed at me and called the girl a whore. He put a curse on her to teach her a lesson. Then, he chased me out of the house and said he was gonna fix me. He tried to stab me with his sword." Frank cooled down, and the two made up, since "Frank and me was lovers."

Frank ordered Paul to steal favors from the merchants in the mall. "If I refused, he got upset. If he saw something he liked, he would tell me to get it for him. He had lots of young kids in the mall steal, too."

The Puz hearing before District Magistrate Wayne Shaffer reconvened on June 5. Linda Clemmer O'Neil linked a T-shirt stained with blood to Atkinson. As the testimony neared completion, Attorney Micacchione moved to dismiss the arson and burglary charges: "There was no evidence presented that Atkinson had entered the premises illegally to remove the copper tub. As a renter, Mike Atkinson had the right to have access to the basement where the tub had been kept."

District Attorney Williams requested all charges be upheld, pointing to numerous other items taken in addition to the copper tub. The magistrate maintained the charges. Following the adverse ruling, Micacchione threw his arms over his head and objected. The theatrics did nothing to sway the court, but they incited his client to react like a wounded Cape buffalo about to be devoured by a hungry lion. Atkinson leapt from his seat and spewed at the magistrate: "This ain't right, I'm getting a bum deal..."

"Mike, sit down and shut up before you get us both a contempt of court citation." Atkinson's outburst had taken his attorney by surprise. The attorney placed his hand on his client's shoulder. "Please, Mike." The defendant returned to his seat like a chastised dog. His big mouth had gotten him in trouble his entire life. His attorney just saved him from another near catastrophe.

Micacchione rose and faced the court to point out errors and inconsistencies in Tom and Connie Hall's written statements and their testimony. The district magistrate overruled the objections and bound over Michael Atkinson for grand jury action on the charges connected with the death of Rosie Puz.

The Kadunce investigation was grueling and time consuming. Chuck trudged home after another long day for some rest and relaxation. Instead, his wife greeted him with a bombshell. "Chuck, I never see you, and when I do we don't communicate. I want a divorce."

"Sandy, I'm bushed. I just finished a long day. Can't we think about this and discuss it later?" Chuck, a confrontation avoider, went to bed that night knowing his marriage had tanked.

The next day, the investigation continued to take center stage. Twenty-six-year-old Raymond "Bluejay" Singer, the brother-in-law of John Dudoic's sister and a participant in a scuffle Abraham broke up years earlier, told the police that Kadunce and Costal may have known each other. During the summer of '78, Bluejay was gabbing with John Dudoic and Frank Costal by the Papermill Bridge on the Neshannock Creek when a red car approached. A mid-sized man stepped out of the vehicle and spoke with Frank and John for several minutes. Bluejay believed the man to be Lou Kadunce, but he wasn't sure.

Thirty-five-year-old Sandy Kroessen claimed to have seen Costal and Kadunce together in 1979, when she lived on Mills Way. On one occasion, she visited her neighbor Donna Thomas, who introduced her to Frank Costal and Larry Kadunce. The four of them sat in the apartment and had a cup of coffee. Sandy left and returned later. She asked Donna if Larry Kadunce was the husband of the woman who was murdered, and she said he was.

Gig and Chuck felt certain about Mike Atkinson's involvement in the Kadunce murders. Strong evidence pointed to the guilt of Frank Costal and Lou Kadunce as well.

On July 6, the detectives re-interviewed Patrick Bowers in the presence of his father. The boy described a June 1978 meeting at the Burger Chef restaurant. "Frank was talking about a Kathy and that her husband was a faggot, and he would like to have him as a gift." Mike Atkinson was there, too, and he said he would like this Kathy as his girlfriend. Frank also called Kathy a "bitch."

Multiple charges and conflicting accounts complicated the cases against Atkinson and Costal. The district attorney asked for more time to prepare. The 180-day rule guaranteed a trial within six months of arrest. The prescribed time was set to expire on August 9, unless extended by the court. The trial had been scheduled for June 23, but pre-trial matters had yet to be completed. The district attorney requested additional time for preparation. Judge William Balph agreed to rule on the request prior to the end of July.

With his mind engrossed by the investigation, Chuck spent even less time with his wife, fourteen-year-old daughter, Barbie, and eleven-year-old son, Chuck. The intensity of the job tore his marriage apart.

"Chuck, I've thought about this divorce all week. We don't have a real marriage. I want out. You can keep the kids while I figure out what I'm going to do," Sandy blurted out that night. A growing emptiness gnawed at the sergeant's stomach. The hint of a tear formed in his eye, but he refused to cry. His job had taken the starch out of him, but Chuck continued to pour himself into his work.

"Chuck, you look beat," Gig noted the next morning.

"Yea, it's been a rough week. Sandy's leaving me, and I can't really blame her. I've been too wrapped up here."

"Why don't you take some time off? Maybe you two can straighten this out." Gig knew Chuck and Sandy were having problems.

"Maybe later," Chuck said, but he knew it was too late. Within ninety days, the marriage ended in a no-fault divorce. Chuck remained a bachelor for more than a decade. He eventually remarried and learned to relax at home by sitting quietly at his workbench and rebuilding antique watches.

In early August, Gig hauled in twenty-one-year-old George Koziol, a nervous little guy who lived with and had sex with Costal for several weeks in September 1978. He had witnessed Costal and Atkinson kissing and Frank selling Mr. Bowers a long-barreled small-caliber gun. Frank had warned Koziol to keep his mouth shut about happenings at his apartment. "Frank told me that if I ever told anyone about what went on at his house, I had better dig a grave and throw myself in it, because if I did not, he would do it for me. I am very scared of Frank, cause he has powers, and he could put a curse on me."

Thirty-three-year-old Dennis Vogan, a frequent drunk-and-disorderly culprit, spent January 1980 in jail with Atkinson. The two prisoners argued over Judy Zook, a woman both men had dated. Vogan called Atkinson an "asshole" and walked away from him. A few days later, Atkinson told a group of prisoners about using a pistol in a killing. Most of the guys assumed he was just bragging and ignored him.

"A couple of days later, I was talking to Atkinson, and he asked me how he could get out of this shit," Vogan continued. "At the time we were talking about the Kadunce murder. I asked him if he did it, and he said he did, but he did not stab anyone. He told me he had sold the gun to a black guy that lived in Crescentdale. He said it was a .22. After that we just quit talking to each other."

When Chuck's daughter, Barbie, invited a couple of her girlfriends over to the house, a handful of teenage boys gravitated to the get-together. Two of them, Jeffrey Wade and Kevan Delaney, told Barbie they had information pertaining to the Kadunce case. She asked her dad to come home from the detective bureau.

Chuck drove the boys downtown for questioning. Wade, a baby-faced fifteen-year-old, claimed to have spoken to Costal at the mall:

Frank the devil man came up and asked me for a light. I talked to him a lot. I heard the rumor he was involved in the murder by Fast 'n Friendly. I just come out and asked him if he was involved. He told me they were going to go where the husband was working and ask him where some dope was. He said they decided to go to the house instead and work over the wife to make her tell about the dope. He didn't say how they got in the house. He said the other guy, I can't remember his name, started to beat on the wife to make her tell, and she wouldn't, so the other guy stabbed the lady. He said there was lots of blood from the baby and the mother. I asked if anyone heard the lady yelling, and Frank said it was early in the morning, and Fast 'n Friendly was closed. After he told me what happened, he started to laugh real loud. He said the cops think the husband did it. They think he is crazy because of Vietnam.

Eighteen-year-old Kevin Delaney described a visit to Costal's apartment in detail: "It was dark with colored lights and speakers all over. Frank told us about the devil and sacrifices and knives. He said when they do a sacrifice, they lay the person on a rug with a star on it, and they stab the person…"

"How many times do they stab the person? Could it be seventeen times?" Gig prodded, leading Kevin through the interview.

"Yea, they stab the person seventeen times starting from the neck down." Since both victims had been stabbed seventeen times, Gig assumed the number might have had some mystical significance.

"How do they get the victims to cooperate?"

"They give them drugs to put them in a trance. He told me he witnessed a sacrifice one time, but wouldn't say where or when it was," Delaney continued, a bead of sweat forming above his eyes. Jeffrey Wade and Kevin Delaney drew an interesting portrait of Costal, even though much of their testimony might not be admissible in the courtroom.

Nineteen-year-old Derek Fuqua, who found himself in jail in March 1980 on charges of criminal trespass, asked Costal about the murders:

I was going to jump on him for killing the baby. He stated he didn't do it, but was there as a witness to the killings by Michael Atkinson. He told me he must have blacked out at the sight of all the blood. I believed what he told me and didn't jump him.…I found out who Michael Atkinson was, and I went to his cell and asked him why he killed the baby. He told me he didn't know why he did it. I grabbed him and threw him down on the floor and kicked him on his head and stomach. While I was kicking him, Atkinson said he didn't do it. After I left his cell, Atkinson ran up to a guard bleeding and said someone jumped him, and he was put in the sick cell. That was the last time I saw Atkinson.

Toward the end of August, the defense attorneys petitioned Judge Balph for a change of venue due to the massive amount of media coverage. Additionally, Attorney Micacchione placed three pre-trial motions before the court:

1. The authorities arraigned Atkinson forty-two hours after his arrest. Pennsylvania law stipulates arraignment must occur within six hours of arrest, a violation of the unnecessary delay rule.
2. Arraignment must occur in the county where the arrest was made. Atkinson had been arrested in Beaver County and was arraigned in Lawrence County.
3. Witness Raymond Thompson should be declared mentally incompetent, having sustained a head injury affecting his memory and reasoning power. All statements he made should be rendered inadmissible in court.

On August 31, while the attorneys awaited an answer to the pre-trial motions, Frank Costal escaped from the Lawrence County Jail with fellow prisoner Edmund Shibble. Throughout his imprisonment, Costal had complained of a variety of real and imagined ailments. He reported a pounding sensation in his chest, a symptom often preceding a full-scale heart attack. Since Costal had a history of heart problems, the guards segregated him from the general population along with twenty-seven-year-old Edmund Shibble, who had been accused of burglary. As the guards escorted the two prisoners to the showers, another prisoner flew into a rage, disrupting the entire jail.

A guard ordered Shibble and Costal to return to their cells and lock the doors. "I'll check on you as soon as this ruckus is taken care of." The prisoners went back to their sleeping quarters but left the door unlocked.

In the morning, Shibble whispered to Costal: "How's about taking a little walk?" He pointed to the unlocked door. "When the shift changes, we can follow the guards out the door. What do you say?"

"Why not. This place sucks, and I got nothing to lose." Costal ached for a taste of freedom, a breath of summer air.

When the guards changed shifts at noon, the prisoners slipped through the open cellblock door. The admissions officer, Clifford Pollock, spotted the uniformed escapees and wrestled Costal to the ground. Costal, a bear of a man, bolstered by the adrenaline of freedom, overpowered the smaller officer. Within minutes, an alarm blared and a cordon of officers initiated a manhunt in the area surrounding the jail. City and state police joined the sheriff's deputies in the search.

A handler brought the escapees' shirts to a bloodhound. The dog sniffed, groaned and led a posse through the neighborhood. By two o'clock in the afternoon, the dispatcher at the station had received several calls about sighting the prisoners along Epworth Street.

Chuck received a call at home from a female friend, who heard about the escape on her police scanner. Chuck snatched a Kent from his bed stand and lit up. He had spent Saturday night hitting the bars trying to forget Sandy and felt in no shape to drive. "You've got to pick me up."

Spotting a uniformed cop, he asked his friend to pull over to the curb. "What's going on?"

"Not exactly sure, but two prisoners escaped. I understand they're just a few blocks from here, and we should have them both soon."

Abraham sobered. He turned to his driver: "I have to head back home for my gun. Then, I need to stop at the station to pick up a radio. Okay?"

"Sure," she answered, eager to take part in the excitement.

While Chuck headed home, the bloodhound caught the scent of the escapees. The dog yanked on its leash and dragged the trainer toward Dean Park. Around 3:00 a.m., the police spotted their prey along Union Street. A brief pursuit followed, culminating in a capture before Chuck had time to return.

"Okay, assholes, don't give us any trouble," a deputy ordered. "Cuff them both."

The men raised their hands. "Hey, take it easy. We ain't gonna cause no problems," Shibble answered.

Costal tried to make light of the escape when questioned. "Everything sort of just happened. I was just following the other guy out the door. I didn't plan nothing. Besides, I didn't try to run away from you guys after you caught up to me." The judge treated the escape with the utmost severity, slapping the prisoners with a two-year sentence.

As September rolled in, the district attorney and Sergeant Abraham attended a yard sale at the home of Costal's sister and her husband, Beatrice and John Gulish. They discovered a plastic skull and a book on the supernatural. When they asked Gulish how much he wanted for them, he gave them the items for free. Gulish allowed the authorities to confiscate three of Costal's swords for analysis, but he wanted them returned. Chuck issued a receipt.

Abraham scrounged through the piles of household effects until he eyed a cardboard container of Costal's books on Satanism, witchcraft and black magic. "How much for the box?"

"I don't know. I guess they aren't worth much. How's about fifty cents?" Gulish answered. Abraham handed the seller a dollar and told him to keep the change.

At the Beaver County Jail, twenty-six-year-old Frank O'Neill described his relationship with Atkinson. "I knew Mike for a period of years. When I saw him in the can, he wanted me to lie for him and be a witness at the murder trial."

Atkinson told O'Neill: "You've got nothing to lose, and I'll make it worth your while. Besides, they aren't going to check or nothing." With enough problems of his own, O'Neill wisely refused.

Attorney Micacchione filed a motion to sever Atkinson's trial from Costal's. The attorney told the *Ellwood City Ledger*: "Costal's escape from jail and subsequent recapture might prejudice the jury against his client." Costal's attorney, Robert Barletta, also sought a separate trial, citing John Atkinson's alleged bribe of Tom Shaffer, a key witness, as a reason. Judge Glenn McCracken approved separate trials, although both defendants had been processed together through the grand jury and preliminary hearings.

The court set the date of September 8 for the completion of "discovery," providing time for the defense to examine the prosecution's evidence.

Complicating the upcoming trial, the Pennsylvania State Disciplinary Board had suspended Attorney George Micacchione for neglecting the cases of his clients. Chief Justice Walter Eager of the state's supreme court ordered the attorney to notify clients of his suspension, allowing him just thirty days to clear up his caseload.

On September 12, just prior to the trial, Judge William Balph held a closed session with Mike Atkinson and George Micacchione in the presence of the defendant's parents to discuss the upcoming suspension.

"Mr. Atkinson, are you aware there are proceedings against your attorney pending before the state disciplinary board, and I also believe the Pennsylvania Supreme Court, regarding suspension and possible disbarment? That is, he would be prohibited from practicing law."

"Yes, I understand."

"Have you heard, Mr. Atkinson, what the reasons are for the action of the disciplinary board against Mr. Micacchione? Do you understand the meaning of that charge?"

"No, I don't."

Attorney George Micacchione.
Lawrence County Bar Association.

"Mr. Atkinson, it has been claimed Mr. Micacchione has neglected his clients' cases. Do you understand the meaning of that charge?"

"I understand."

"It also has been charged, and you must understand I'm not commenting upon whether the charges have any basis whatsoever, that he has made false statements concerning that neglect. Did you know that?"

"No."

"I would say this to you, Mr. Atkinson, do you realize these charges made against an attorney cast doubt upon the honesty of such an attorney? Do you understand that?"

"Yes," Atkinson answered.

"Do you also understand that because these charges have been made against your attorney and have been publicized in the newspaper, a jury might not consider Mr. Micacchione to be a believable and honest attorney? Do you understand that risk?"

"Yes."

"Do you think Mr. Micacchione can and will handle your case competently and honestly?"

"He's about the only one in this county I do trust, and I believe he can do it."

The judge proceeded to catalogue the adverse publicity on Micacchione's charges during the past several weeks. Atkinson answered: "They can't be no worse than mine. I don't believe ninety percent of the stuff that's in the *New Castle News.*"

With Atkinson's acceptance of Micacchione as his attorney of record, the first trial for the murder of Dawn and Kathy Kadunce began.

10

THE ATKINSON TRIAL

A one-week selection process impaneled twelve jurors and two alternates, all sequestered at the Holiday Inn in nearby West Middlesex to guarantee Mike Atkinson's unbiased trial, untainted by the news media or public opinion. The county anticipated an expensive trial. In addition to legal costs, the court budgeted $11,000 to pay for transportation to and from the courthouse, hotel rooms, breakfasts, dinners and around-the-clock protection employing multiple shifts of guards and tipstaffs.

Glenn McCracken, a distinguished judge in his late forties with dark curly hair and a broad face outlined by wire-rimmed spectacles, clad in the traditional black robe of office, formally convened the proceedings on a balmy sixty-degree Thursday, September 25, 1980. That very day, Chevy Chase had referred to Cary Grant as a "homo" on the *Tomorrow* show, leading to a $10 million defamation suit. Back in New Castle at the Lawrence County Courthouse, the judge instructed the jury regarding the Commonwealth's case against Mr. Atkinson: "Ladies and gentlemen of the jury, you have been selected to perform one of the most solemn duties of citizenship, to sit in judgment on charges made by the Commonwealth against one of your fellow citizens. You should pay close attention to what is said and to what occurs throughout the trial."

The judge cautioned the jurors against discussing events with one another, reading, listening or viewing any media that might refer to the trial or the defendant and could affect the outcome of the case. Mike Atkinson, sitting at a table beside his attorney, unshackled to avoid influencing the jury with

Right: Judge Glenn McCracken.
Lawrence County Bar Association.

Opposite, top: Courtroom Number 3.
Author's collection.

Opposite, bottom: Lawrence County
Courthouse. *Author's collection.*

any presumption of guilt, stared toward the front of the courtroom with stone-cold eyes. Once the judge completed the instructions, he nudged his glasses along the bridge of his nose and recessed the jury for the balance of the day.

Tuesday morning opened with a bus ride to the Wilmington Avenue crime scene. After a tour of both floors and the outer perimeter, the jurors returned to the courthouse, where the trial began in earnest. District Attorney Don Williams, a Sunday school teacher and elder in his church, called his first witnesses. Rose Butera and her daughter, Lori Gingas, provided background evidence on their discovery of Dawn and Kathy Kadunce's bodies. Brian Baer, Lori's one-time boyfriend, offered further information. Officer Arthur McGuirk, Anthony DeCarbo of DeCarbo Ambulance, County Coroner Howard Reynolds and Dr. William Gillespie provided physical and medical evidence regarding the state of the bodies of the deceased, creating the necessary chain of evidence to prove the occurrence of a murder.

Wednesday involved additional physical testimony. Officer Ron Williams identified photos of the Kadunce house. State policeman Lester Strawbridge ran through the fingerprint and blood analysis performed by the laboratory. Recently retired police officer George Kennedy identified twenty-two items

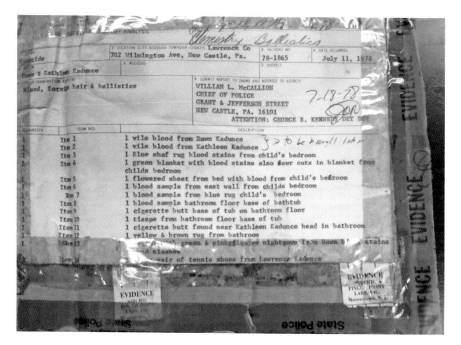

Evidence from the crime scene sent to Erie for testing. *Courtesy of the New Castle Police Department.*

turned over to the state police in Erie for testing. He introduced Dawn's bloody blanket, nightgown and bed sheet into evidence. The day ended with Erie criminologist John Robertson discussing hair, blood and fiber trace elements taken from the Kadunce house.

The opening salvo pleased the prosecution. Like a mason, skilled in the use of brick and mortar, District Attorney Don Williams constructed the strong foundation needed to cement the conviction process.

The third day kicked off with city engineer Alphonso Rozzi, who presented a scale drawing of the Kadunce home. Thirty-one-year-old Larry Kadunce took the stand as the tenth witness in the trial to the murmur of voices droning throughout the courtroom. He had difficulty with simple questions like the birthdates and the ages of his children. "I get mixed up," he replied, trapped in the maze of legal mumbo-jumbo.

Sensing Kadunce's nervousness, the district attorney coaxed the information from him. The witness recalled attending New Castle Business College the Monday evening prior to the death of his wife and daughter. He left class early to cash a check at the Giant Eagle supermarket, returning home in time to watch *20/20* on television.

District Attorney Don Williams.
Lawrence County Bar Association.

The D.A. asked what he did the morning of July 11.

"I woke up, and I gave the baby a kiss. He was in the crib, and…"

"Where was the baby kept?"

"In the doorway entering our bedroom." The D.A. knew Rose Butera discovered the infant downstairs the day of the murders, not in the bedroom.

As the questioning continued, Kadunce fidgeted. He explained, "I kissed the baby, and I…Since Dawn was a light sleeper, I was hesitant to go in and kiss her for fear of waking her up. I went down the stairs, got dressed, and I went out to the car. I started it and pulled around to the front of Fast 'n Friendly next door to get a Pepsi and cigarettes, but since I was picking up my nephew, I was running late, and the store was not open yet…"

"What time was that when you went outside to start the car?" The D.A. interrupted.

"Twenty to seven."

"Did you talk to Kathy?"

"I don't really know whether I talked or not, because she was breastfeeding the baby at the time and throughout the night."

"Do you normally keep your doors locked?"

"Yes," Kadunce answered.

Prosecuting officer Sergeant Charles Abraham watched and listened from his desk, seated beside the district attorney, following the ebb and flow of the answers. He recorded his thoughts on a notepad. His sense of order and sheer persistence usually delivered the correct answers. He remembered Rose's testimony that Kathy always locked her door and jotted the fact on the pad.

"Did you lock up that morning, Mr. Kadunce?"

"To the best of my knowledge I did."

After getting in the car, Kadunce noticed he was low on gas. He backed out the car and left to pick up his nephew. "Usually, we play jokes on each other, and I beeped the horn and decided to pull around the corner and come around again, but as I was pulling away, I saw his wife in the window, and I knew the joke was over. They already knew I was there, so I pulled around the corner and came back, and Ron got in the car."

Chuck listened closely while doodling on his pad. He thought the witness had more to say about his route. If running late and low on gas, why would he take the time to play a joke on his nephew? On the other hand, he also questioned whether someone involved in his wife and daughter's deaths could possibly think about playing a joke on his nephew. After purchasing a Pepsi at Lawson's and gas at Big Bear, Kadunce arrived at work around 7:30 a.m.

Chuck remembered a friend telling him the word *testimony* came from Latin. Since the Roman courts preceded the coming of the Bible, a witness held his testicles and swore on his manhood. Chuck snickered to himself as he envisioned Kadunce grabbing his balls while lying.

Although Chuck hoped the D.A. would continue his line of questioning on the route, the attorney shifted direction. The cop shrugged his shoulders and continued taking notes.

The D.A. passed the witness to the defense. George Micacchione slowly rose from his seat and made his way to the stand. As his questioning intensified, Kadunce's voice dropped several octaves. "Just a moment," the judge interjected, "Mr. Kadunce, will you speak up?"

"Yes, I will try, Your Honor. I have had the same problem in school, not speaking up. It's not intentional."

"Okay," Micacchione continued to pressure the witness. "Now, on your statement it states you went down to the Fast 'n Friendly. Then you drove to Highland Avenue by way of an alley?"

"Yes."

"Trying to get gas?"

"Yes."

"Is that the closest station?"

"No."

"Isn't it true, Mr. Kadunce, if you were so low on gas you easily could have gone a couple blocks up Wilmington? Isn't there a Workingman's Gas Station right up the road?"

"Yes, there is."

"But instead you went over to Highland. Where did you go from Highland?"

"Down Highland, downtown."

Micacchione asked Kadunce to map out the remainder of his route to work. Although an early statement to the police shortly after the murders indicated he went to the gas station prior to Lawson's, his courtroom testimony stated the opposite.

The judge interrupted:

> *Just a minute. Ladies and gentlemen of the jury, there have been inconsistent statements upon which the witness has been cross-examined. Now when a witness makes a statement which appears to conflict with or contradict testimony at trial, you may consider evidence of the other statement in deciding whether or not to believe the witness's testimony, but that is the only purpose for which you may consider it. Let me give you an example unrelated to this trial. Suppose a witness testifies in trial under oath that six shots were fired. Then, the witness is shown a prior inconsistent statement he made before the trial and out of court wherein he said two shots were fired. Now, this is the only thing the jury can do. That prior inconsistent statement about two shots is not to be considered, because it was made out of court. The statement about two shots being fired can only be considered in considering whether the witness is telling the truth at trial when he said six shots were fired. Now there is a statement that he thought he stopped at Lawson's first and the gas station second. So you can only consider a prior inconsistent statement if you believe it impeaches the credibility of what he said in court about the order of the stops at Lawson's and the gas station.*

Micacchione asked to approach the bench for a sidebar, a conversation between the defense, prosecution and judge outside the hearing of the jury. "I would take exception to the court's charge given to the jury just now. I don't believe this is the law anymore in Pennsylvania, Your Honor. There have been several recent supreme court decisions which indicated that prior inconsistent statements may be considered as evidence in and of itself without going to the credibility of the witness."

The judge declared a recess to check the law before making a ruling. When the court reconvened, the judge reversed his earlier position.

Having won his point, Micacchione picked at other memory lapses and inconsistencies made by the witness.

Kathy Kadunce was not wearing her rings when her body was discovered. The husband claimed to have found his wife's blue star sapphire ring and wedding band in a glass on the mantel in the living room, turning them over to his mother-in-law. However, two photos taken by the police shortly after the discovery of the bodies failed to show a glass sitting on the mantel.

Kathy Kadunce's wedding band and blue star sapphire. *Courtesy of the New Castle Police Department.*

From the first day he had been assigned the case, Attorney Micacchione recognized the uphill battle he was facing. His client's dark and brooding eyes presented a menacing look—a nearly insurmountable obstacle. His strategy must be to convince the jury that Atkinson had been falsely accused through his own bravado. He intended to point the finger of guilt at the husband, who, spurred by jealousy or other motives, had acted alone. His questioning continued.

"Did you and your wife have any problems, other than ordinary problems?"

"Yes, we did."

"Didn't you have some type of confrontation with Mrs. Anastasia, your landlord's wife?

"I had a confrontation with her."

"Wasn't this due to the fact that you took the garbage out in the altogether?"

"If you're talking about whether I took out the garbage in the nude, yes, I did. I have that problem. I was seeing a psychiatrist, and I still see one."

"You were in the county jail for it?"

"Yes."

"When was that?"

"I can't remember the dates."

"Can you approximate it?"

"Maybe a year, two years."

"What year was it?"

"I don't remember."

"1973, 1974, 1975, 1976?" Micacchione ticked off the dates, indelibly etching them in each juror's mind.

"I don't really remember."

"Was Dawn born while you were in jail or not?"

"I don't remember if she was born. I think I asked the judge to let me out so I could see my daughter being born, but I don't know really."

"Do you recall, Mr. Kadunce, how long you had been in jail?"

"Approximately a month, month-and-a-half." Mr. Micacchione relished the witness's discomfort, dangling before the jury like a worm on a fishing hook.

Attorney Micacchione requested a five-minute recess to obtain a certified copy of the incarceration dates from the prothonotary Helen Morgan's office located on the first floor of the courthouse. Documentation proved Kadunce had been jailed from December 27, 1973, through February 19, 1974. Micacchione changed his line of questioning.

"Isn't it true you were discussing your problem with exposing yourself on the morning of July 11, 1978, Mr. Kadunce?"

"No, it is not." The husband bristled at the accusation.

"Was there ever a discussion that Kathy was going to leave you?"

"The last discussion I remember was when she was going to leave me was way back when we lived on Crawford Avenue."

Micacchione next tackled Kadunce's proficiency with firearms, a skill he picked up while serving as an air force security policeman. Lou testified to owning .22-caliber ammunition but no gun. In fact, he denied ever owning a pistol.

George Micacchione, a suave Duquesne University graduate with neatly groomed hair, dressed impeccably and boasted almost a decade of legal experience. His striking appearance and knowledge of the law coupled with a natural aggressiveness that could push a witness into contradicting

MASTER
11-12-73   78

UNITED STATES DEPARTMENT OF JUSTICE
FEDERAL BUREAU OF INVESTIGATION
IDENTIFICATION DIVISION
WASHINGTON, D. C. 20537

The following FBI record, NUMBER 121 420 MB , is furnished FOR OFFICIAL USE ONLY. Information shown on this Identification Record represents data furnished FBI by fingerprint contributors. WHERE DISPOSITION IS NOT SHOWN OR FURTHER EXPLANATION OF CHARGE OR DISPOSITION IS DESIRED, COMMUNICATE WITH AGENCY CONTRIBUTING THOSE FINGERPRINTS.

CONTRIBUTOR OF FINGERPRINTS	NAME AND NUMBER	ARRESTED OR RECEIVED	CHARGE	DISPOSITION
SPol New Castle PA	Lawrence Martin Kadunce D11112	8-13-73	indecent exposure	
SPol New Castle PA	Lawrence Martin Kadunce D-11255	9-18-73	indecent exposure	
SPol New Castle PA	Lawrence Martin Kadunce D11263	10-9-73	Indecent Exposure	
SPol New Castle PA	Lawrence Martin Kadunce D11392	10-31-73	Indecent Exposure	

Lou Kadunce's rap sheet. *Courtesy of the New Castle Police Department.*

his own testimony. His razzle-dazzle tactics revealed Kadunce's confusion and/or lies regarding dates, times and travel routes along with his incarceration for exposing himself. The ploy generated enough doubt to avert the pressure from his client and to offer up another suspect for the jury to consider.

In contrast to Micacchione's effervescence, the district attorney, Don Williams, a balding, slow talker, dressed in a rumpled suit, presented a folksy style. However, he was a skilled litigator and a Duke University law graduate, who rarely stood in front of the witness, preferring to post himself beside the jury box, forcing the jurors to center their attention on the witness. He never badgered but led each witness in his chosen direction with carefully worded questions.

Listening to Kadunce's answers for more than five hours left Abraham nearly brain dead. He picked up a copy of the *New Castle News* to take his mind off the trial, but the paper held little in the way of positive news. Iran had bombed the Iraqi oil fields. President Jimmy Carter insisted that the Straits of Hormuz must remain open for commercial traffic. Ninety-year-old Rose Kennedy suffered from an intestinal obstruction requiring surgery. She would recover and lived past age one hundred. Even the sports page was a bummer, reading "Bucs Virtually Dead." Chuck Tanner's Pirates sat four-and-a-half games behind Philadelphia with only nine games to go. They did not make the playoffs that year.

Back at the courthouse, Pennsylvania state trooper Virgil Jellison, a ballistics expert, identified the .22-caliber bullet fragments found on the floor of the Kadunces' bathroom—probably fired from an inexpensive foreign gun based on the bullet's grooves.

"Slim" Williams testified to buying a .22-caliber pistol with a crack in the barrel from Mike Atkinson on a Sunday afternoon in July 1978. Micacchione asked whether it might have been June instead of July. Throughout Slim's testimony, Mike chattered in his attorney's ear.

"Quiet Mike, I can't concentrate on what he's saying," Micacchione scowled.

Mike muttered something under his breath. Within minutes, he interrupted his attorney again. Juror number six stared at the defendant and shook his head. Sergeant Abraham noted the outburst on his pad, realizing Atkinson's temperament could only help solidify the conviction process.

The defense questioned Williams.

"This particular gun, you indicated it was broken?"

"The barrel was broken."

"Could the gun have been fired in the condition it was in?"

"It might have, but I wouldn't have tried to fire it if you would have given me $1,000," Williams answered. The police attempted to recover the pistol using a metal detector. They slipped Williams's young son five dollars in the process to help. The hunt turned up nothing of value. When Williams explained that his son begged the police to continue the search a second day so he could earn another five dollars, a snicker of laughter passed through the audience.

Next, Cheryl Buckel testified that her sister Kathy Kadunce smoked marijuana around 1972.

"Was it as a result of meeting Lou Kadunce?" Micacchione asked.

"In my opinion, yes."

"Did she break away from this use of marijuana?"

"Yes, she did. When she was pregnant, she didn't do it after that."

"Did Lou continue to smoke after this time period?"

"After '73, yes."

"Was he smoking in '75, '76, '77 and '78?"

"I don't know. Well, now in '75, yes, because that is when the other incident happened." Cheryl was referring to Lou exposing himself and his subsequent incarceration.

"You have seen Lou smoking marijuana?"

"Yes, sir." The defense turned to Lou's military career.

"Was Lou ever in combat to your knowledge?"

"No."

"Wasn't he wounded, Cheryl?"

"Self-inflicted. He shot himself in the leg. There is a picture of it in the album. As far as I know, that is what I was told about it." Micacchione's cross-examination focused on Lou's drug use, psychological problems and the self-inflicted wound, tainting his character.

Thirty-three-year-old Dennis Vogan provided information on his interaction with Atkinson while both served time in the Lawrence County Jail and their discussion on the Kadunce killings. Mike questioned how he could get out of this mess.

"I asked him if he done it."

"What was his reply?" asked the D.A.

"He said he shot her, but he didn't stab her." Vogan's statement conflicted with that of Jane Garcia, who had claimed during an early interview that Costal had shot Kathy Kadunce.

"Was there any discussion about a pistol?"

"He told me he sold it to a black man that lived down by Wampum somewhere, Carbondale."

Micacchione cross-examined Vogan to impeach his testimony. He asked why he waited until August before telling the police what he knew since his conversation with Atkinson occurred the prior January. He also pointed out the witness's grudge against the defendant.

"You and Mike had some words, didn't you?"

"Yes, we did,"

"And was the statement made before or after the argument."

"After."

"Why would he do that?"

"I don't know. People in jail just confide in people."

"Mr. Vogan, why would he want to know how to get out of this mess when he wasn't charged until February 9?"

"I don't know." Micacchione continued to poke holes in Vogan's story.

Ex-con nineteen-year-old Derek Fuqua, a tall, militant African American awaiting disposition on a robbery charge, sauntered to the witness stand.

"Me and a few guys went to Mike's cell and asked about the murder of the baby."

"You all went to his cell?" the D.A asked.

"Yes. I asked him why he killed the baby."

"What was his answer?"

"He said he didn't do it."

"And what did you do then?"

"Threw a biscuit at him." The courtroom snickered. The judge struck his gavel for quiet.

"What did Mr. Atkinson do after you left his cell?"

"Ran to the guards."

"Why did he do that?"

"Because he was hurt." Williams relinquished the witness to Micacchione.

"Mr. Fuqua, when you gave your statement to the police, did you tell them you kicked Mike Atkinson?"

"Yes."

"Did you tell them you kicked him in the head?" Micacchione waved his arms and raised his voice for effect.

"Yes."

"Did you tell them you kicked him in the stomach?"

"Yes."

"Were you charged with that?"

"No."

"Isn't it true, Mr. Fuqua, you are presently serving a sentence for receiving stolen property?" Micacchione wiped his forehead and awaited an answer.

"Yes."

"Mike Atkinson never said one word about killing anybody, did he?" Micacchione shouted.

"No."

"You took it upon yourself to be the enforcer of the jail?"

"No."

"Did you tell the police you grabbed him off his bunk?"

"Yes."

"Mr. Atkinson was removed from the cell block because of what you did. Isn't that correct?"

"Yes."

"Did you plan and organize it?"

"Nope."

"Did you intend to kill him?"

"No."

"Isn't it true you made this statement, because you were told charges would not be filed against you?"

"Nope."

"Did you ask the police to do anything to help you out?"

"Yes."

"What did you ask them to do?"

"Help me in court."

"Is that the reason you made this statement?" Micacchione prodded.

"No."

At sidebar, Micacchione requested the court file charges for assault against Fuqua.

"What has that to do with this trial?" Judge McCracken snapped.

"I am concerned with justice."

"It has nothing to do with this trial. I am not directing the D.A. to do anything," the judge barked, obviously irritated with the defense's smokescreen.

The D.A. called officer Mike Lastoria, who reviewed the police procedures employed in obtaining Atkinson's February 10 statement taken at the Butler County Jail.

During cross-examination, Micacchione criticized the facts of the statement, the methods used to obtain it and the sloppiness of the investigation.

"Sergeant Lastoria, where was Jim Antoniotti on July 11, 1978?" Atkinson's original statement had placed him at the crime scene on the day of the murders.

"He was in prison." Antoniotti had been incarcerated at Western Penitentiary for burglary. Micacchione suggested Lieutenant Frank Gagliardo used duress to force Antoniotti's and Atkinson's false statements. He questioned how the police failed to interview the boy named Paul mentioned by Atkinson. He pointed out that Antoniotti had a seventeen-year-old son named Paul. The lawyer asked why the police never followed up that lead, implying that Jim Antoniotti might have lied about his involvement to protect his son.

Darlene Pounds, a one-time girlfriend of the defendant, testified that Atkinson moved out two or three days after the Fourth of July.

"During that time, where did he work?"

"He didn't work."

"While he was there, did you ever visit any other cities with him?"

"We went down to where his sister lives, Mount Pleasant."

"When was that?"

"I think around June 11." Mike's alibi placed the couple in Mount Pleasant the day of the murders. The tiny town in Westmoreland County had once been an important coal center. In 1891, more than one hundred workers died during an explosion in the Frick Corporation's Mammoth Mine, located just six miles from the city square.

"During the time he stayed with you, did you know of him having any firearms?"

"He had a gun that I know of."

"How did you become aware of it?"

"He pointed it at my head."

"Did you ever visit Frank Costal's house?"

"Yes."

"And what did you see there?"

"Objection, Your Honor, irrelevant," Micacchione protested.

"We'd better have a sidebar," the D.A. countered. The D.A. stated that Pounds saw artifacts of a satanic cult. The judge questioned the relevancy. The D.A. explained that he intended to tie in human sacrifice rites and Satanism to the murders.

"Human sacrifice rites?" questioned Judge McCracken. "Do you propose that to be connected to the homicide?"

"Yes, we do," the D.A. insisted.

Micacchione objected. "This stuff can't go in because if it comes in now, and there is no connection shown, we have got a mistrial. It is merely meant to inflame. The only way it can be shown is the particular wounds on the body. If that stab wound is consistent with ritual performances, then I say he could do that. We have already heard from Dr. Gillespie, who did the autopsy, in his opinion these were unrelated to any kind of cult or human sacrifice."

"He didn't say that," the D.A. snapped.

"He certainly did," the defense attorney fired back. Micacchione and Williams had fought each other tooth and nail for days. The pressure had reached a boiling point.

"Well?" the judge asked the D.A.

"We will withdraw these questions until we lay further foundation." The D.A. opted to hold the cult theory in reserve. The sidebar ended.

Micacchione examined Darlene Pounds, attacking her recollection of the dates, but she remained firm. The defense revealed the fact that Mike had beaten the witness, presenting the argument that Pounds held a strong enough grudge to risk perjury.

"You never called the police for that."

"No, I didn't."

During redirect, the D.A. asked, "Were you afraid of him?"

"That's the reason I didn't call the cops." The court day ended.

The next morning, Lieutenant Dan Malley of the New Castle police corroborated Darlene Pounds's story in which she stated that the car Atkinson supposedly drove to Mount Pleasant was not drivable after July 4. He answered a call to retrieve the keys from Atkinson, who refused to return them to Pounds. His testimony went a long way to contradict Atkinson's alibi of being in Mount Pleasant on the day of the murders.

William Howley, a teacher at the Youth Development Center, told the jury his friend Lou Kadunce had served as a sergeant in charge of air force security at Pham Rang in Vietnam. Micacchione prodded the witness into describing Kadunce's leg wound as intentional, but Howley failed to confirm such a conclusion.

"Did Mr. Kadunce ever partake in the use of drugs while he was in Vietnam?"

"I'm not sure exactly what you mean by the use of drugs."

"Marijuana?"

"Yes," Howley answered hesitantly.

"When he came back to the states, did he continue to use marijuana?"

"I'd say yes to some degree."

The defense switched its line of questioning.

"Were you aware of any marital problems?"

"I was aware they had a marital problem at one time."

"Did this have anything to do with Mr. Kadunce's problem regarding exposing himself?"

"I believe so."

Attorney Micacchione ended his examination with a parting salvo: "Isn't it a fact, Mr. Howley, during the discussion of incidents you had in Nam, the shooting in the leg sometimes came up?"

"I'm sure it would."

"In the course of discussing this incident, it was often stated this was a self-inflicted wound, is that correct?

"Yes."

"No further questions." Micacchione continued to point his finger toward the husband as the prime suspect.

Thirty-year-old Ron Silvis verified the times and routes taken by him and his uncle, Lou Kadunce, on the day of the murders. During cross, Micacchione asked, "By the way, Mr. Silvis, when did you make a pass at Kathy Kadunce?"

"In March of '77." This allusion to a brief affair left the jury with a prime motive for Lou Kadunce, jealousy.

Throughout Silvis's testimony, Sergeant Abraham, the prosecuting officer, sat quietly, tapping the point of his pencil against the table, taking notes or drawing stick figures during sidebars. He attempted to look busy, adjusting his tie, pushing back his hair, doing anything to avoid distracting the jury. He recognized that Atkinson made a lousy appearance with his swarthy coloring, glaring eyes and cockiness. Even when the defense scored points, Chuck believed the jury would convict Atkinson.

The D.A. summoned to the stand Eileen Rizzo, Kathy Kadunce's mother, a clean-cut lady with a dignified demeanor. "Did problems come up with Kathy as to whether she would continue living with Lou?"

"Yes, she called me the day he was arrested, and she was crying. She said, 'Mom, Lou's in jail.' I asked her, 'What for?' At first, she wasn't sure, because he had said he was held up, and they made him lay in a ditch or something, and they made him take his clothes off. Evidently, he got back in the car. They let him go. They held a gun to him was the story she told me, and they let him go back to the car. He supposedly stopped these children to ask them a question or something. They say he had exposed himself to them, and she asked me what she was supposed to do, and I said that if she couldn't accept the problem to leave him before she had any more children, but if she loved him to stick it out. She decided to stay with him."

Twenty-six-year-old Robert Grim, a bulldog of an inmate awaiting sentencing for breaking and entering, sat before the jury to answer questions from the D.A.

"Was Mike Atkinson in your cell block?"

"Yes."

"And did you talk to him after he got there?"

"We got to playing cards together."

"Did any discussion come up about the Kadunce affair?"

"I asked how his case was doing. He told me he had it beat. He said these people really didn't know what they were doing. Then I asked what he meant. He told me the gun used, he had sold to a kid's father on the north block with us, but he said these people here got it all screwed up. The dates were wrong and everything as to when he sold the gun."

"Did he talk later about it?"

"Well, he thought he could beat it. When he told me about the gun, I was beginning to think he had done it, so I tried to stay away from him, but he was bothering me about a guard he paid off, and if he could get a gun and bust out."

"Objection," called out the defense.

"On what grounds?" asked the judge.

"Irrelevant to the situation and not part of the statement."

"Objection sustained." The judge instructed the jury to ignore the last statement.

"All right, did Mike say more about the Kadunce matter?"

"He told me her husband had given him the key, and he was to do what he had to do because she was supposed to get out of the house and wouldn't leave." Mike whispered something into his attorney's ear.

"What did he say he did?" The D.A. stared at the jury box to emphasize the answer about to follow.

"Well, there was a mock trial, and lots of guys were getting on Mike about being a baby killer. He kept hollering for the guards. He got pretty emotional. He wanted the guys away from the cell, so the guard come back and broke it up, and Mike told me, 'I didn't kill the baby. I didn't do that part. Frank did that.' Then, he admitted killing the mother."

During cross, Micacchione asked, "What part did you play in this little mock trial?"

"I was the judge."

"You did sentence him?"

"Yes, I did."

"What did you sentence him to?"

"Death." The courtroom reacted with gasps and whispers.

The judge banged his gavel and announced, "We won't tolerate outbursts from the audience."

"You attempted to carry out that sentence, didn't you?"

"No, I did not."

"Other inmates did at your direction?"

"No, they did not."

"Why did Mike get all emotional?"

"Because he was scared."

"What were you doing throughout all this, Mr. Grim?"

"I guess I was getting on him, too."

"You were jumping on him, yelling at him, weren't you?"

"I wasn't jumping on him."

"Your determination for finding him guilty, was that based upon what you thought you knew?"

"Yes."

"Mike likes to be the center of attention, doesn't he?"

"Yes," the witness answered. Mr. Micacchione painted Atkinson's confession as the idle boasting of a liar and a braggart.

Atkinson's eyes shot daggers at the hotheaded Paul Pounds as he walked toward the stand. Pounds glared back at the defendant. The two men had nearly come to blows after Mike and Darlene Pounds's separation.

"Do you have a sister Darlene?" the D.A. asked.

"Yes."

"Do you know where she lived in the spring of 1978?"

"She lived on Jefferson Street."

"Do you know where Mike Atkinson lived in the spring of 1978?"

"Yes, he lived at the same place."

"With your sister?"

"Yes."

"Did you know Mike to carry a hunting knife?"

"Yes."

"What type?"

"A regular hunting knife."

"How did he carry it?"

"On his belt." Sergeant Abraham made a note on his pad. He remembered Atkinson's original statement in which he claimed Pounds carried the knife.

During cross-examination, Micacchione demonstrated a practical reason for Mike carrying a knife. "Mr. Pounds, when Mike would wear this knife, did he use it to go fishing?"

"He used it to cut the fishing line, stuff like that."

During recross, the defense chipped away at the witness's credibility. He asked Pounds about his stay on the fifth-floor psychiatric ward of the St. Francis Hospital. "Isn't it a fact you were in the hospital, because you have a sudden nature to become violent?"

"I wouldn't say that. I went there on my own."

"Did you punch out a window as a result of your behavior?"

"I punched out windows before."

"No further questions." Having implanted Pounds's lack of mental stability into the jury's consciousness, attorney Micacchione sauntered back to his seat.

Twenty-eight-year-old ex-con Richard Garr testified to his knowledge concerning a pistol used by Atkinson in the murder. Speaking in a thick Spanish accent, he stated, "When they asked him if he knew where the gun was, he said he never would tell them where it was."

"Did he ever say anything about them finding where it was?" asked the D.A.

"He said they never would find it unless they....What can I say in English? When they check the water, what do you call that? Okay, it's like when they scrape the bottom to look for it." The witness had difficulty describing the dredging of a lake for evidence.

"Well, what about anything else?"

"That a knife was involved."

"Did he ever associate himself with being a hitman?"

"Yes, sir."

"What did he tell you?"

"He would fulfill contracts that were given to him."

"All right. That is all." The D.A. glanced toward the defense table. Micacchione rose, positioned himself in front of the stand and spoke slowly and methodically.

"Mr. Garr, when did you talk to Mr. Atkinson?"

"About the second day he was there"

"Mike was trying to impress everybody, isn't that right?"

"Yes, sir."

"He was telling everyone what a big man he was?" Micacchione recognized discrediting Atkinson might be a key element in gaining an acquittal.

"Yes," the witness agreed.

"Were you under any type of medication when you gave the statement?"

"Yes, sir."

"What kind of medication?"

"Dilantin." Physicians used Dilantin with phenobarbital as a calming agent.

"Now, in the statement made by Mike Atkinson, didn't he tell you the woman was raped?" Micacchione knew the autopsy had demonstrated no indication of rape.

"Yes," Garr answered. Micacchione chalked up a key point. Sergeant Abraham silently grimaced. He imagined how good a cigarette might taste.

"Did Mike Atkinson state anything about the woman being shot?"

"No, sir."

"Did he ever talk to you about killing the woman or just raping her?"

"It was rape."

"Isn't it true that in the statement the only thing he mentions about the woman is the fact that it was rape."

"Yes, sir."

"You indicated you thought Mike was trying to impress you?"

"Yes."

"What do you mean by that?"

"Well, most of the guys come in the jail and put on a big show."

"A lot of the stuff is not true?"

"Yes." Atkinson shuffled in his chair throughout Garr's testimony. His attorney disrespected him, as if he were not even in the room. He did not like people to mock him.

"They just do this so they can be the big man in the block?"

"Yes, sir."

Attorney Micacchione brought up witness Garr's institutionalization for drug use. "What hospital were you in?"

"Northside," a hospital located in Youngstown.

"Any particular ward?"

"One East."

"Is that a general ward?"

"Do I have to answer that?" Garr looked toward the bench.

"Yes, you do," the judge ruled.

"For drugs and alcohol," the witness mumbled. "I was there because I had too many drugs in me, and they didn't know if I was going to make it or not, so I was put on the isolation ward for an overdose."

"Have you been in the hospital for anything else beside barbiturates?"

"Just convulsions."

"No other drugs?"

"No."

"No acid?"

"I used to take it."

"What are you referring to?"

"Powder windowpane."

"Windowpane acid?"

"Uh-huh."

"What kind of effect does windowpane acid have?"

"It's a hallucinating drug."

"How does it come?"

"Little strips." Abraham noted the mileage lining Garr's face.

"What do you do with it?"

"You put it in your eyes, or you can swallow it." Attorney Micacchione raised his bushy eyebrows and glanced toward the jurors. They seemed to have little or no familiarity with drugs in general and windowpane acid in particular. Garr's drug addiction combined with his story concerning a rape might cause the jury to discount his entire testimony.

Chuck whispered to the D.A., "Shouldn't you object?"

"Shh, I know what I'm doing." Williams felt the opposing attorney's constant haranguing might backfire. The jury, and Chuck along with them, had begun to sympathize with the witness.

Stacy Reed, a short woman in glasses, followed Garr to the stand. She recalled seeing two men disappear in the woods behind her house a few blocks from Fast 'n Friendly around 7:30 a.m. on the day of the murders.

"Later on, did you meet either of these people?" the D.A. asked.

"Yes," Mrs. Reed answered.

"Where?"

"At an apartment."

"Whose?"

"Frank Costal's."

"Where was that apartment?"

"On Highland Avenue by Reynolds Funeral Home."

"Did you go alone?"

"No, never alone. I was there with Randy Perrotta."

"When you saw Frank Costal at his apartment, did you recognize him?"

"Yes, I recognized him as the other man who came down the hill that morning."

"You may examine."

The D.A. motioned toward Micacchione. After adjusting his tie, the attorney approached the jury box and fired his opening question: "Do you recall testifying at the preliminary hearing?"

"Yes."

"Do you recall testifying about whether or not when you met Frank Costal at his apartment you recognized him?"

"No, I don't recall that."

"Let's see if we can help you recall. Let the record show I am presenting defendant's Exhibit B, a transcript of the preliminary hearing. I call your attention to pages 456, 457, 458 and ask you to read those pages, please. Do you recall that testimony, Mrs. Reed?" The attorney pushed the statement in front of the witness and allowed her time to read.

"Little bits of it."

"Do you recall, Mrs. Reed, you testified when you met Frank Costal, you did not recognize him as the person who came down the hill that day because you never thought about it?"

"No, I recognized him as the person I seen coming down the hill when I first met him. I didn't put anything together until after I had seen what was in the paper." Attorney Micacchione continued to punch holes in Mrs. Reed's testimony as a reliable witness.

"Do you recall the question at the top of page 456? Question: 'And when you met him, did you recognize him as one of the individuals?' And your answer was: 'No, I didn't even think about it.' Question: 'And it never occurred to you until after you saw he had been arrested for this particular crime that it was him, is that correct?' Your answer was: 'Yeah.'"

"That's what I said there."

"Isn't it a fact, Mrs. Reed, that at the same time you saw Frank Costal's picture in the paper, you also saw Mike Atkinson's picture in the paper?"

"I'm not sure. I remember seeing Frank's picture in the paper."

"You're not sure," he repeated, emphasizing the words "not sure."

"I don't…unless it was beside it. I don't know."

"Even at that time when you recognized them, you didn't go to the police, did you?"

"No, because I was afraid."

"Were you afraid of Frank Costal?"

"I don't know exactly what I was afraid of. I had two children. That gives me reason enough."

"Are you working now?"

"Yes."

"Where?"

"Bailey's Restaurant."

"Who is your employer?"

"Dee and Frank Bixler."

"Anybody else?" Abraham cringed. He hoped Micacchione would halt this line of questioning to avoid the discovery of any potential impropriety, since he had suggested to his mother-in-law, Dee Bixler, that she hire Stacy Reed as a waitress in her restaurant.

"No, that is who hired me."

No further questions. Abraham breathed easier, relieved to escape any embarrassment.

After a brief examination, the D.A. passed the witness back to Micacchione for redirect. The defense challenged Stacy Reed's identification of Costal and Atkinson. "Will you tell us now when you saw Frank Costal at his apartment, did you or did you not recognize him as the man you had seen on the road?"

"I recognized him as the man coming down the hill."

"Did that have any significance to you at that time?"

"No, it didn't, you know, other than I had seen him coming down."

"Was there any point later that it did become significant to you?"

"When it came out in the paper he was arrested for murder." Stacy Reed stepped down from the stand.

The D.A. called Sergeant Charles Abraham, who laid his pencil on his pad and stepped up to the stand.

"Sergeant Abraham, will you tell us, did you visit Mike Atkinson on the thirtieth day of January 1980?"

"Yes, I did."

"Where did you find him?"

"It was at the Lawrence County Jail," the witness blurted. As soon as the words left his mouth, Abraham knew he had blundered. His answer implied that Atkinson had been incarcerated on other charges.

Attorney Micacchione pounced on the error. "If it please the court can I have a sidebar?"

Abraham's revelation provided ammunition for a mistrial. The testimony might cause the jury to assume that the defendant had committed another crime prior to the one for which he had been charged, jeopardizing his right to a fair and impartial trial.

As Micacchione approached the bench, the hint of a smile crossed his face. Like a ravenous lion tasting blood, he pounced. "I move for a mistrial. The district attorney asked the witness where he went to see Mike Atkinson and when. He said the thirtieth day of January 1980, in the Lawrence County Jail. It has already been stated that Mike Atkinson was not arrested for this particular charge until February 9, 1980. Therefore, the jury might infer he was in jail for some other instance."

Judge McCracken frowned. The D.A. and the police sergeant made a bush-league slip-up. He looked weary as he declared a recess, adjourning to his quarters to meet with the defense, prosecuting attorney, the defendant and a stenographer. After considering the pros and cons of Micacchione's pleading, the judge ruled to void Sergeant Abraham's previous testimony and continue the trial. McCracken felt the jury missed the impact of Sergeant Abraham's revelation. After a strong censure from the court, Abraham returned to the stand.

The D.A. requested him to play the tape of Atkinson's statement of February 10, 1980. The tape opened with Abraham reading Atkinson the Miranda rights as proscribed by law. Then, Atkinson described the evening prior to the murders.

"Okay, July 10, 1978, I was at Halco Drive at Jim Antoniotti's house, and there was Judy Antoniotti, Paul, Paul Pounds, Bobby Hall, Bobbi, Frank and I, regarding a drug we was supposed to have come in on, acid, and something went down that a…Kathy was supposed to have ripped us off."

"Kathy who?"

"Kadunce."

"So arrangements were made where I picked up Frank, Paul Pounds, Judy Antoniotti and I."

"When was this supposed to take place, what time?"

"Early in the morning. It was around quarter to seven."

"So when I picked up Frank, Paul Pounds was already there. We left from Frank's and crossed over the side streets past Fast 'n Friendly and down over by…like a dirt road to Judy's house. So there was Frank and I and Paul in the car. When we got to Antoniotti's, we picked up Judy and Paul."

"Do you know this Paul?"

"No."

"What did he look like? How old would he be?"

"Fifteen."

"Okay, go ahead."

"We left Judy Antoniotti's house. We went through the back door, got in the car. Frank, I and Judy sat in the front. Paul Pounds and this young Paul sat in the back, and the understanding was when we got to Kathy's house, young Paul and Frank was going to roughen her up to tell where the drugs were."

"When you parked your car, where did you park it?"

"On the side of Fast 'n Friendly."

"Okay, who got out of the car?"

"Frank, Paul Pounds and young Paul."

"Were any carrying weapons that you could see?"

"Not offhand. Paul Pounds does carry a hunting knife. He also has access to a .22, Italy-made, Saturday-night special, seven shot."

"Do you happen to know if he had these weapons with him that morning?"

"Not that morning. I know he always carries his knife, but I don't know about his gun."

"Did you see the knife on him?"

"Yeah, tied to the right side of his belt."

"You said they went into the house, which house did they go into?"

"I can't be sure if it was the first, second or third house, because all the fronts match."

"Okay."

"After they went in, I asked Judy if she wanted a cup of coffee. I went in Fast 'n Friendly, and instead of coffee, I got two cans of soda. I came out. We sat there, smoked a couple cigarettes. About fifteen minutes, twenty minutes, maybe half an hour later, Paul Pounds, Frank and this young kid Paul came out."

"What did they look like when they came out?"

"When Paul Pounds came out, he didn't have his T-shirt on. He had his Levi jacket on, and I asked him where his T-shirt was. He said he just threw it away, but Frank had something red on his jacket. I asked Frank what it was, and he said, 'Red paint.' I said, 'Are you sure, because it looks like blood.'"

"Where at on the jacket?"

"His right arm."

"Did he have what looked like blood on him when he left the car?"

"No."

"What was said when he got back in the car?"

"When they got back into the car they said, 'Well, we have fixed her. She told us where the acid was.' And everybody was supposed to meet back at Judy Antoniotti's house later that night to get their share of the acid."

"What happened after they got in the car?"

"We went over to Judy Antoniotti's house. I dropped off Judy and this kid Paul, dropped off Frank downtown at the post office and Paul Pounds at the south-side projects."

"Okay."

"After I dropped off Paul Pounds at the one project, I went home."

"Did they say they killed her?"

"No."

"When did you learn she was murdered?"

"About a week later through the papers."

"Did you have any feelings or was anything said to you that you might have thought they were killed?"

"No."

"Do you know now what happened?"

"Yes, because I'm being charged for it."

"Were you threatened in any way to make this statement?"

"No."

"Are you afraid of us in any way?"

"No, just afraid of being done in."

"By who?"

"If word gets out I made this statement."

"Are you willing to testify to this?"

"Yes."

"In other words, you realize you are putting yourself in jeopardy, but you are still willing to testify?"

"Yes, because at the time it happened, I told them I didn't want no felony raps. That's why I didn't go into the house." The playing of Exhibit 115C for the jury concluded.

"Sergeant, did you interview the defendant any further following the eleventh day of February?" the D.A. asked.

"Yes, on the twelfth of March," Abraham answered.

"What did he tell you that differed from these statements?"

"Nothing, other than he mentioned about what happened to the gun."

"What did he tell you?"

"He told me he had sold the gun to a party by the name of Slim Williams in Crescentdale."

"Did he tell you why he was talking to you?"

"He said he could give us Frank Costal on a silver platter." Two jury members shifted in their seats.

"Is there anything further?"

"He mentioned something about not even being there. He said he was in Mount Pleasant on that date, and when we confronted him with facts that he was seen in town, he changed his statement. 'Well,' he said, 'there is no point in trying to lie out of it. I was there.' Then he went on about being in the car and not going inside."

"Now, sergeant, you talked to the defendant in the morning of the tenth of February prior to the time you took that statement, is that correct?"

"Yes, sir."

"What if anything did the defendant tell you at that time as to the car?"

"On the morning of February tenth, he gave me a verbal statement, and it was basically the same as the taped statement of that evening. The only difference was that he stated he had used his father's blue Mustang. When we came back that evening, he switched from the blue Mustang to an avocado station wagon."

Williams turned over the witness to the defense for cross-examination. Questioning centered on a pistol Mike supposedly stole from a woman in Prospect in May or June 1978.

"After he had gotten the gun, what did he do with it?"

"He said he had given it to Frank Costal. Frank had used it and gave it back to him and told him to get rid of it."

Micacchione leaned on the stand and pressed the sergeant, pointing out inconsistencies between the statements made during the preliminary hearing and the present trial. He shoved his face into the witness's space, spraying saliva and raising his voice with each question. "I'm going to ask you one more time, sergeant. During the course of the conversations with Mike Atkinson regarding…"

Judge McCracken interrupted after observing the defense's aggression. "Just a moment, counsel, unless you have something to point out to the witness such as a transcript or a written piece of evidence, please question him from the table. Let the record show counsel is leaning against the bench, talking in a loud tone and pointing his finger at the witness." Thus chastised, Micacchione returned to his seat and grabbed a sip of water to cool his ardor.

Proceeding with his cross, Micacchione attempted to lure the cop into an admission that Kathy might refer to Kathy Laux, Frank Costal's niece, rather than Kathy Kadunce. "Did you ever talk to Kathy Laux?"

"Yes."

"Is she related to anybody involved?"

"She is related to Frank Costal."

"And did he mention her before Kathy Kadunce?"

"No, he didn't."

"Who mentioned the name Kathy Kadunce, you or Atkinson?"

"Atkinson."

"When?"

"On my first interview with him."

"You went for what purpose?"

The witness paused. He appeared reluctant to answer and stammered, "Which time are you talking about?" The D.A. requested a sidebar.

"Approach the bench," the court ordered.

The D.A. explained, "The first interview contains suppressed evidence, and I cautioned this officer not to say anything about those times. It is giving him difficulty, possibly revealing he talked to the defendant prior to the twenty-eighth of January, and he knows those matters were not to be put in evidence."

"What is your position, Mr. Micacchione?" queried the judge.

"I intend to have him answer the questions I'm asking."

"Even if it deals with a suppressed matter."

"I don't care if it deals with a suppressed matter or not. If I'm asking the questions, I will go into it,"

"What is the law if the matter has been suppressed? Can the defendant nevertheless use it?" The D.A. sought a clarification.

"Yes, I can use it. It's my choice," Micacchione argued.

After more give and take, the court asked, "Who moved it to be suppressed?"

"The defendant," answered Micacchione.

Judge McCracken declared a recess to check the appropriate legal precedents on suppressed evidence. When court reconvened in chambers, the judge sized up the opposing lawyers. D.A. Williams asked questions with a soft country twang combined with the zeal of a preacher schooled in the canons of right and wrong. In contrast, the urbane and flamboyant, but effective, George Micacchione, attacked opposing witnesses like an angry pit bull, bullying them into potential conflicts and errors. Both men were extremely competent and knowledgeable in the law.

Looking at the two gladiators, the judge dissected the suppression issue with surgical precision. "As I understand it, Commonwealth witness Sergeant Abraham has been asked questions by defense counsel, the answer to which comes from interviews which have been suppressed pursuant to defendant's motion, is that correct?"

"That's correct," replied the D.A.

The court ruled Micacchione had the right to question the witness on suppressed matters during cross-examination. However, the judge cautioned, "The defendant can't complain later about it, because it is a situation he created."

When the trial recommenced in open court, Micacchione quizzed Sergeant Abraham on the affidavit of probable cause. "And the date upon which you swore to this affidavit of probable cause is what?"

"Ninth of February, 1980."

"You filed this affidavit of probable cause to get a warrant prior to taking these two statements, is that right?"

"That's correct."

"On January 30, when you took Mike Atkinson's statement, he told you James Antoniotti went into the house, didn't he?"

"Yes, he did."

"And he was present with two other people."

"James Antoniotti was present with two other people."

"What is an affidavit of probable cause?"

"It's an application to get an arrest warrant."

"And you have to state what you have been told, what you believe, isn't that right?"

"I believed it."

"Didn't Mike Atkinson tell you to talk to James Antoniotti, and he will verify everything?"

"It wasn't those words. He said go pick him up. He will be scared. He will tell."

"You believed Jim Antoniotti when he said Mike Atkinson went inside that house, right?"

"Because he verified what Mike Atkinson told me."

"Why would Mr. Antoniotti admit to being at the scene of a crime when he was in jail the day it was committed, and he couldn't be involved?"

"I don't know what his reasons were. I attempted to find out after we found he was in jail. He wouldn't talk."

"What investigation did you run?"

"We called the penitentiary that day, or Larry Turner, the parole officer, called to verify he could not have been out on some kind of leave."

"Now, after learning this, did you file an additional affidavit of probable cause?"

"Yes, we did."

"You took an oral statement, a written statement and a taped statement on the evening of the tenth, correct?"

"Yes."

"Why did you come back the eleventh?"

"To clarify about Antoniotti being there."

"Why did you need another statement? You already had two?"

"To see if he would tell the same story again."

"He told you the same story on January 30. How many more statements…"

"He told the same story, but somebody else was playing the role of Jim Antoniotti."

"On the thirtieth of January?"

"On the thirtieth of January and on the tenth of February, Mike had Antoniotti in the picture. On the thirtieth of January and on the tenth of February, he had the blue Mustang in the picture…in the morning. In the evening, he switched to the avocado-green station wagon. On the eleventh, he switched to Paul Pounds from Jim Antoniotti," the sergeant explained.

"Did you ask him specifically why the car was switched?"

"He said, 'There is only one thing I lied about, the blue Mustang. I was in an avocado-green station wagon.'"

"What else do you want clarified? Let's get it all out, sergeant." Micacchione peppered the witness with sarcasm. Abraham recognized the attorney neither liked nor respected him, and he reciprocated the feelings.

"I really don't know," Abraham answered uncertainly.

"You really don't know? Didn't you want something clarified about a gun?"

"What gun are you talking about?"

"The gun that was supposed to be used in this crime."

"He told me he sold it to Slim Williams."

"He didn't tell you that until March 12."

"That's correct."

Micacchione's questions struck with pistol precision at the inconsistencies between the Atkinson and Antoniotti statements as well as the affidavit of probable cause. "You did read the affidavit before you signed it?"

"Yes, I did."

"You swore the information in it was true and correct, is that right?"

"I believed it to be true and correct."

"Did you believe Dawn Kadunce died on July 11, 1979?"

"No, it was 1978. That was a typographical error."

"Not only did you miss it once, you missed it twice. Didn't you?"

"That's correct."

"Might I ask you why in the first tape you had to advise Mr. Atkinson of Mr. Costal's name?" asked Micacchione, his hands perched on his hips.

"If I remember correctly, he said Frank Batzel. Then I clarified it, and I asked if that was the same person as Frank Costal, and he said yes."

"Why didn't you ask him if he goes by any other name rather than mentioning the name yourself?"

Micacchione's voice grated on Abraham like fingernails scraping across a chalkboard. The sergeant had spent the better part of the day on the witness stand. To disguise his anger he gulped in a breath of air and answered in calm, controlled tones. "It was more or less a relaxed interview when I was talking to him."

At the conclusion of Sergeant Abraham's testimony and the retirement of the jury, Micacchione requested a dismissal of all charges, arguing:

> *The defendant did not with premeditation, and that is the distinguishing factor, kill or have cause to slay one Kathy Kadunce. We aver that the evidence put forth is insufficient to sustain murder in the first degree. In regard to the slaying of Dawn Kadunce, again, the defendant with premeditation did not cause the death of Dawn Kadunce. There is nothing to connect the defendant with the slaying of either one of these two individuals. Taking the evidence as presented by the Commonwealth, it shows a gun was gotten rid of, that he drove someone with the idea they were going to rough Kathy up, but he did not go into the house. He was not present when anything occurred. He was in the parking lot in a car, and he drove away.*

Micacchione argued further:

> *Dan Marley is of no relevance. Mr. Howley is of no relevance; Mr. Silvis, no relevance; Mrs. Rizzo, no relevance. Mr. Grim claims Mr. Atkinson said Kadunce gave him the key to get her out of the house, but he didn't kill the baby. Mr. Garr states Mr. Atkinson again said he had nothing to do with the killing but spoke about a contract for rape. Stacy Reed is only relevant to the fact that she claims she saw Mike Atkinson sometime between 6:30 and 7:30 a.m. walking with Frank Costal down Boyle's Avenue Extension. I submit to the court her testimony should be discounted, because it is the impression of counsel she didn't really see what she said she saw. All she saw was two people walking down that particular street. She could not identify whether they had any weapons; she could not identify whether they had any blood on them. Miss Callahan, her testimony does not shed any*

light on this matter, and then we have Sergeant Abraham, who testified regarding tapes and how the tapes were taken. The Commonwealth doesn't produce the man who made the statements resulting in the arrest of Mike Atkinson. Abraham said he believed him, and the officer again said he believed Stacy Reed, and he believed Mike Atkinson. We would submit to the court on the basis of the record there is insufficient evidence to hold this defendant and allow this decision to go to the jury. I would make the same motion relative to all four charges, Your Honor.

"All right, Mr. Micacchione. Mr. Williams?" The judge asked the D.A. to respond.

"If the court please, this Commonwealth has shown through many witnesses there was a *corpus delicti*. The evidence is so clear there is not much point of making an argument. The Commonwealth has produced witnesses to show this defendant was associated with a co-defendant."

The D.A. proceeded to enumerate the litany of evidence placing the defendant at the scene of the crime.

Sergeant Abraham and others indicated he had put himself in the area. He put himself in the planning stage the night before. He put himself there with testimony showing his clear-cut appreciation of the scene. Now, under the doctrine of Commonwealth versus Hartman, when a defendant gives conflicting statements about material matters, this in itself is indicative of guilt. This defendant gives a statement as to the car he was using. It would be argued by defense counsel the testimony of Darlene Pounds doesn't prove anything. It proves he was not using the green car he said he was using on the 10th of July....I think he is deliberately lying, and a jury can well conclude he is guilty, the guilty person who killed both of these people, or did it through an accomplice in a joint venture. We seek it be submitted to the jury for that purpose.

After reviewing both arguments, Judge McCracken denied Micacchione's motion to dismiss the charges.

As Chuck Abraham departed the courtroom following a tortuous day, the tipstaff approached him and commented: "You must have the memory of an elephant to remember all that stuff." Chuck smiled and kept moving. He had stayed up late the previous evening to review Atkinson's interviews and his notes. Tonight, he planned to reward himself with a few well-deserved drinks.

Sergeant Charles Abraham prepares for testimony. *Courtesy of the New Castle Police Department.*

The next morning, Attorney Micacchione opened the defense by calling Preston Currie, an inmate at the Lawrence County Jail and a witness to Mike Atkinson's mock trial.

"Who was the leader of this particular trial?"

"Robert Grim."

"Did Mike and Grim get along?"

"No. Grim was always on his back, you know, talking about his case, that he killed the people."

"Did Mike ever say to him that he did it?"

"Not that I can recall, no."

"Did you ever have a conversation with Robert Grim regarding the information he had given to the district attorney?"

"He said he needed something to get out of jail, so he was going to testify to get out of jail and get the charges dropped."

"And did he tell you what he was going to testify to?"

"No, he just said he was going to say Mike was in on the killing."

"Since that particular time, have you had any further discussions with Robert Grim?"

"He said he wasn't going to sign the statement he had written, then the cops kept coming over. Finally, he said he was going to sign it."

"I have no further questions." Micacchione flipped a page from his notes to signal his completion.

Micacchione next called John Atkinson, the defendant's father, a ferret-faced man with darting eyes, who described the trip he took to Mount Pleasant for a visit with his daughter in the early part of July 1978. The witness claimed Mike and Darlene Pounds had been with him on the date of the murders. Sergeant Abraham eyed the senior Atkinson, a liar and a moral bankrupt. The cop felt certain John Atkinson had taken part in the Puz robbery and murder but allowed his son to take the fall.

"When did you go to your daughter's house?" asked Micacchione.

"We went on Friday night, July 7….I was there for my birthday."

"When was your birthday?"

"June 29."

"When you went on July 7, with whom did you go?"

"Michael and his son, Darlene and her two older kiddos. They went in Darlene's station wagon. I went in my car."

"That means he would have left New Castle on July 7 and returned to New Castle on the fourteenth of July. Is that correct?"

"It was the fourteenth when I come back. The next day was the fifteenth. I got my fishing license. I remember that." Assigning a specific event to the date painted the testimony with a veneer of truth. Abraham assumed John Atkinson had been coached to affix this point. The issue boiled down to whether the jury believed the testimony of Atkinson's father or the contradictory input of Darlene Pounds. Abraham raised his eyes from his notepad, scowling at the witness, certain the jury would recognize John Atkinson's statement as perjury, a Hail Mary coverup to save his son.

Micacchione next called on the defendant, often a dangerous tactic. Mike Atkinson swaggered forward. Juror three crossed his arms and scrutinized every step the defendant took toward the stand. Early questions to the witness led to obvious discrepancies, distortions or obvious lies. His attorney attempted to mask the answers in a smoke screen.

"Do you know Jim Antoniotti?"

"Yes, I do," Atkinson answered. Sergeant Abraham assumed the jury shared his disgust for this psychopathic degenerate, thief, rapist and murderer.

"Do you know Judy Antoniotti?"

"Yes."

"Did you attend a meeting at Antoniotti's residence on Halco Drive on July 10, 1978?"

"No," Atkinson responded, contradicting his statement given in February. Abraham shook his head in disbelief at the lie.

"Did you know Kathy Kadunce?" Micacchione continued.

"No, I didn't."

"Did you know Larry Kadunce?"

"No, I didn't."

"You made some statements to the police, did you not, Mr. Atkinson?"

"Yes, I did."

"And in your statement, you talk about Kathy's sister?"

"Yes."

"Who is Kathy's sister?"

"Marge Baker."

"And who is Kathy?"

"Kathy Laux." Abraham wondered how the defense expected the jury to swallow this garbage.

"Kathy Laux, is she any relation to Frank Costal?"

"It's his one niece."

"And Marge Baker, is she any relation to Frank Costal?"

"Yes, it's his other niece."

"The morning of July 11, 1978, were you driving a vehicle within the city of New Castle?

"No, not within the city of New Castle."

"Where were you driving a vehicle?"

"Mount Pleasant. I went to the Shaft Club; that's my brother-in-law's." Atkinson tied a second circumstance to his story in an attempt to cement the alibi.

"On July 11, 1978, were you in the presence of Frank Costal?"

"No, I wasn't."

"On July 11, 1978, did you walk into a house at 702 Wilmington Avenue?"

"No, I didn't."

"And shoot and stab Kathy Kadunce and Dawn Kadunce?"

"No."

"Kathy Laux, does she have any children?"

"Yes, she does."

"Boy or girl?"

"She had," Atkinson paused, "uh, in 1978, she had a daughter the same age as my son, Michael, which would have been at that time four. Her daughter's name is Dawn."

"Her daughter's name is what?"

"Dawn."

"D-A-W-N," the attorney spelled out the name to drill it into the jury. Abraham tried to remember the names of Kathy Laux's children but couldn't. He knew the D.A. must be thinking the same thing, and the two would check out this detail later in the day.

"Did you ever know anything about the murder that occurred on July 11, 1978, except for what you read in the newspapers?"

"No, I didn't read that much about it in the newspaper."

"But you gave these statements, did you not, Mr. Atkinson?"

"Yes."

"Now why did you make these statements?"

"I was told to by Sergeant Abraham and Lieutenant Gagliardo when they came to the Lawrence County Jail. They questioned me about this homicide. They told me Kathy, whatever her last name is, I can't pronounce her last name, he told me Laux and her was one and the same."

Judge McCracken saw the jury was having a hard time understanding Mike Atkinson as he mumbled. The defendant explained he had a sore throat. "Well, it's important everybody hears your testimony," the judge interjected.

Micacchione continued: "Why were you transferred to the Butler County Jail?"

"Security, at that time, Sergeant Abraham told me if I didn't make the statements against Frank Costal, he would make sure the inmates would know I was in on the double homicide."

"Did you have some other concerns while you were in the Lawrence County Jail?"

"Yes, I did. My father."

"Where was your father?"

"He was in the south range of the county jail."

"Had you talked to anyone regarding this?"

"Sergeant Abraham."

"What are you talking about?"

"If I went ahead with this, he would have the charge dropped against my father." Atkinson referred to the charge against John Atkinson as an accessory in the Puz murder case.

"After you made the statements, Mr. Atkinson, was your father released?"

"He was released on bond."

"When you talked to the police, you talked to them about being at the meeting at Antoniotti's house. Is that correct?"

"Yes."

"And it was over some acid?"

"Yes, it was."

"And it involves Kathy?"

"Yes, Kathy Laux."

"When was that meeting?"

"1977, June."

"When you made the statement on the eleventh of February, were you told Jim Antoniotti had been in jail?"

"I believe it was the morning of the tenth? It was on a Sunday. Sergeant Abraham told me Antoniotti was incarcerated on a burglary charge of Pete's Bait Shop."

"Were these statements the truth?"

"No."

"Isn't it true, Mr. Atkinson, that you like to impress people?"

"To some extent," the witness answered. He wanted to lash out and explode but knew his attorney was trying to make a point in his favor.

"Isn't it true you open your mouth sometimes about things you really don't know anything about?"

"Sometimes." The witness followed his attorney's lead.

"You like to have a lot of attention paid to you, isn't that true?"

"Not all the time." An undertone of voices circulated throughout the courtroom. The judge struck his gavel for decorum and announced, "We are going to break for recess."

"I have one more question, Your Honor."

"Mr. Atkinson, did you, in July 1978, know Frank Costal?"

"Yes, I did."

"Did you ever receive a key to the Kadunce home from Lawrence Kadunce?"

"No."

"No further questions."

Following the break, Micacchione requested a sidebar prior to passing the witness to D.A. Don Williams. "Your Honor, I request this court instruct the audience there is to be no comment during the jury testimony of this defendant. On direct, various noises emanated from the audience, oohs, aahs and sounds to indicate unbelievability. I would think the court should caution the audience."

Following the judge's admonition for silence in the courtroom, District Attorney Williams questioned Atkinson. The witness claimed he and Darlene had driven to Mount Pleasant, returned to New Castle on July 7, 1978, for Darlene's domestic relations hearing and went back to Mount Pleasant that evening. Atkinson swore he had purchased drugs from Kathy Laux in 1977, not 1978, and she had "ripped him off."

"All right, I would like to show you this statement. We will ask whether or not this is your signature on Commonwealth's Exhibit 114. Now, whose name is that?" The D.A. handed over the statement.

"Mike R. Atkinson," the defendant stammered.

"Did you write that?"

"Yes."

"And did you read the statement?"

"It was read to me."

"Now this part says, 'I wish to make the following statement without fear, threats or promises.' What does that mean to you?"

"Well, like I stated before, at the time I filled that out, I wasn't in my right mind."

"You weren't in your right mind from what?"

"I was under medication."

"What were you taking then?"

"Chloralhydrate dalmanes."

"Let's go back to the question, what does this mean, without fear, threats or promises from the police?"

"I didn't fill the top part out."

"Did you read the whole thing yourself?"

"No, I didn't."

"Was it given to you?"

"It was slidden in front of me."

"I would like to show you Commonwealth Exhibit Number 114A, does it have your signature?"

"Yes."

"It states: 'No promises have been made to me, nor have any threats been made against me.' Do you understand that?"

"Yes."

"Didn't you say here in talking to your defense counsel you were promised something?"

"Yes."

"What were you promised?"

"That my father would be released of charges."

"What does this mean, 'no promises were made,' how do you justify these statements?"

"Well, if I didn't sign, Sergeant Abraham would have me transferred back to the Lawrence County Jail, and he stated Paul Pounds and all of them would be in the same range." Atkinson scowled toward Abraham, who returned a faint smile. By recanting his written statements, Mike hoped his verbal testimony painted Sergeant Abraham and Lieutenant Gagliardo as liars who set him up as a fall guy.

"You took that in the form of a threat, is that right?"

"Yes," the witness snarled.

"It also says here, 'nor have any threats been made against me.'"

"Well, at the time, I didn't have any choice," Atkinson weaseled.

"When you signed that, wouldn't this mean you are telling everybody who reads this no threats or promises were made, is that right?" the D.A. persisted.

"I believe so."

"Then, you lied in the statement, is that what you are saying?"

"Yes."

The D.A. changed his line of questioning. "This statement says, 'On the 10th of July, 1978.' Is there anything the matter?"

"Yes."

"It says you were at Judy Antoniotti's house. Were you?"

"No."

"Well, why did you sign that statement?"

"I didn't read that. All I did was sign it. I believed anything I signed is not legal anyways."

"Well, what does it mean when it says, 'knowing that the same may be used against me in the event of any court action,' what does that mean to you?"

"I didn't understand it at the time."

"What did you think they were asking information for?" the D.A. barreled forward relentlessly.

"Just a statement testifying against Frank Costal."

"Then why did you think they were asking about that?"

"Because of Sergeant Abraham." Abraham looked up from his notepad at the mention of his name.

"What because of Sergeant Abraham?"

"He asked me if Frank had any dealings on Wilmington, or if he ever went that way, and I said, 'Yes, he went that way to Jim and Judy Antoniotti's.'" Sergeant Abraham eyeballed the jury to gauge their reaction.

"In addition to these statements, you made taped statements; you got to hear them, did you not? And then were your rights read to you?"

"Yes."

"And did it say, 'no threats were made against you?'"

"Yes."

"And you are saying now that wasn't true; is that right?"

"Yes."

"On February tenth, you told him Jim Antoniotti was there with you, didn't you?"

"Yes."

"And on February eleventh, you said he wasn't, didn't you?"

"I just didn't put his name back in the statement."

"But you said at that time Paul Pounds went up there with you?"

"Yes."

"Why did you make two different statements?"

"Just...I feel...because at that time he would realize they was false statements." Atkinson struggled to cover his tracks.

"Sergeant Abraham did realize they were false statements about Jim Antoniotti. He did tell you that, didn't he?"

"Yes."

"On the eleventh, you made a different statement and left him out, isn't that right?"

"To some parts, yes."

"But you had different people doing different things?"

"Yes."

The D.A. returned his inquiry to the subject of police intimidation and threats. Atkinson replied, "If I didn't make the tape, I'd be taken back to the Lawrence County. I am only saying what Sergeant Abraham and Lieutenant Gagliardo told me." The witness stumbled over the pronunciation of Gagliardo's name.

"Well, was Lawrence County a bad place?"

"Yes, it was my understanding Paul Pounds was there. Jim Antoniotti was there. Frank Costal was supposed to be there, Judy Antoniotti, her son, Paul."

"Did you ever see any of them in jail."

"Just Frank Costal."

"Are you afraid of them?"

"More or less, yes."

"Why?"

Atkinson shrugged his shoulders and looked down at the floor. "Just certain reasons, I don't believe in fighting." A member in the courtroom snickered, and the judge scowled toward the direction of the noise, unable to pinpoint the offending party. The room immediately became quiet.

"Mike, did you know Mr. Vogan?" the D.A. asked.

"I met him when I came to the Lawrence County Jail."

"Did you have conversations with him?"

"We had words about one girl we used to date."

"By the name of Zook?"

"Yes, we had some foul language going back and forth."

"Did you reconcile those differences?"

"No."

"Did you ever talk to anybody about what you were in jail for?"

"Yes, my attorney and George Robinson."

"Is that all?"

"That is all beside my mother."

"You were transferred to Beaver County....Did you talk to anybody down there about the case?"

"No, except for one party."

"Who was that?"

"Frank O'Neill."

"And over on the jail here you got to know Mr. Garr?"

"I knew him to play cards or to see him."

"Didn't you talk to him?"

"No."

"You just sit there silently when you play cards?"

"I don't talk to many people in that county jail." The D.A. knew the jury would have difficulty stomaching Atkinson's explanation. He paused a beat to allow the jury time to digest this reply before churning forward.

"How about Mr. Grim?"

"Talked to him one time."

"Just one time?"

"Yes. When he started calling me names and harassing me, I just told him, 'I have enough charges on me, leave me alone.'"

"Now, on the tape you were talking about a Kathy Kadunce?"

"I was told her name instead of Kathy Laux's name, and I asked Sergeant Abraham, 'Why can't I just put both names down since it is the same party?'"

"Are you saying that statement was what Sergeant Abraham wanted you to say?" Chuck Abraham stared at the ceiling and twirled a pencil through his fingers to steady his nerves.

"Yes, most of it was what Sergeant Abraham wanted me to say." Atkinson continued to provide ready answers, regardless of their lack of believability. He shot Abraham hateful looks.

"You just make a false statement because Sergeant Abraham wants you to, is that right?"

"Partially."

"Do you like him that well?" the D.A. asked, tossing a baited hook at the witness.

"Can't stand the man since he lied," said Atkinson with a gritty smile, swallowing the barb.

"Well, if you can't stand him, why would you cooperate and say something that's not true?" The D.A. reeled in his prey and dangled him before the jury like a hooked fish flopping on shore.

"The man told me he would help get my father out of jail. I found out later he couldn't have the state's charges dropped."

"I would like to go back to this trip you made and the time you lived on South Jefferson Street. Did you know Lieutenant Malley?"

"Yes."

"Did you see him in 1978?"

"Yes.…He came to my father's house. I believe I still was in bed. He woke me up."

"What did Lieutenant Malley come to see you for?"

"He wanted Darlene's car keys."

"Did you give them to him?"

"Yes."

"Where was the car?"

"Parked in front of 1315 South Jefferson Street."

"Do you know how Lieutenant Malley knew to get the keys from you?"

"Darlene sent him over."

"Do you know whether that was after the Fourth of July or before?"

"I couldn't remember."

"Do you remember where you spent the Fourth of July, 1978?"

"With my father and son."

"And do you know what Darlene did?"

"That day? I believe she was with her sister's boyfriend, Joe Hooks. Darlene was using the car that day."

Empty lot on South Jefferson, where Atkinson lived in 1978. *Author's collection.*

"Did you live with her the day before the Fourth of July?"

"Yes."

"That is the last time you ever lived there, wasn't it?"

"No, it wasn't."

"Do you have any idea whether she went to a hearing on the seventh of July?"

"No."

"But you contend you drove her all the way back from your sister's to come to a hearing?"

"To see her husband about a hearing. That is all she told me."

"And what was the purpose in her seeing her husband?"

"Something about support, I guess. Darlene never told me the truth the whole time. That is why we broke up."

"Did she pay the rent?"

"No, I did."

"When did you last pay the rent on the house at 1315 Jefferson?"

"July 3."

"And what month was that for?"

"July."

"Did you ever pay any rent after that?"

"Not to my knowledge."

"As a matter of fact, you didn't stay there after the third either, did you?"

"Yes, I did."

The D.A. shifted gears. "Now, Mr. Atkinson, are you saying these people who stayed with you in jail are not telling the truth?"

"I didn't tell them anything."

"Did they talk to you about your case?"

"They asked me questions about it. I told them to mind their own business."

"And you even asked to be taken somewhere else?"

"Yes."

"Well then, these statements you made on February the tenth, wouldn't they have caused you a great more trouble?"

"In which way?"

"With the people in jail?"

"Probably no."

"Wouldn't you have more fear of them than you would have of Sergeant Abraham?"

"Never thought of it that way."

"Had you known Sergeant Abraham before this time?"

"Yes."

"And were you afraid of him?"

"Not really."

"You aren't afraid of him now, are you?"

"Not as long as he is sitting there."

"And you weren't afraid of him when you made these statements, were you?"

"No, but he did make promises."

"And you are saying the statements are false and everything you said on the tape was false?"

"Yes."

"And you are saying Darlene's seeing your sister in June of 1978 is false?"

"Wasn't in June 1978. It was in July of 1978."

"And you are saying your having moved out of that house at 1315 South Jefferson in early July is false?"

"Late July," the witness corrected. "I would say it was between the seventeenth and the twentieth."

"And you are saying it was false that you received a key from Lou Kadunce for his house?"

"Yes."

"And you are saying it is false that you ever went there?"

"Yes."

"And you are saying it is false that you killed those people?"

"Yes."

"Well, is there ever any time we can believe what you say?"

"What I said here today is true."

"How do we know which statement you make is true and which is false?"

Attorney Micacchione leaped to his feet and objected: "Your Honor, it is calling for a conclusion on the part of the witness to make a determination of what the district attorney should think."

"Objection overruled," the judge announced. "Could you repeat the question, Mr. Williams?"

"I will reword it. How is anyone supposed to know when your statements are true?"

"About the same that you would Sergeant Abraham." The D.A. recognized both the judge and jury's growing impatience with the witness as he continued his examination.

"Do you know of any way of providing us with a means of knowing when you tell the truth and when you don't?"

"I believe I have witnesses here today."

"You mean when your statements are supported by someone else, then you would want us to believe them, is that right?" A titter of laughter emanated from the rear of the room.

"Yes."

"Well, if the only way we can tell when your statements are true is when somebody else backs them up, shouldn't we just listen to them instead of you?" Abraham thought how much Gig would have liked to watch Atkinson squirm.

"I'm going to object to this line of questioning, Your Honor," Micacchione interjected.

"Can you rephrase the question, Mr. Williams?" the judge asked.

"Then, the only time we can find out whether your statements are true is to go on other witnesses. Is that right?"

"Yes."

"So your statements don't help at all?"

"I don't know if they do or not, but what I said here today is true," the witness insisted.

"Do you know any other way we can get at the reliability of your statements?"

"I was believed by my attorney at one time or another. He asked if I minded taking a polygraph test, and I told him, 'No, I am willing to take one.' In fact, I will take it right here in court."

Despite his outward bravado, the trial had gotten to Atkinson. He was scared. The previous day was his twenty-ninth birthday. Today, the D.A. attacked him on a dozen fronts, and he lacked the words to defend himself.

"That is all the questions we have, Your Honor." The D.A. backpedaled from the witness like a ditch digger with dirty hands, anxious to shower and clean up after a hard day's work. Micacchione immediately requested a sidebar.

"Your Honor, there was a gentleman standing in the back who when the jury entered the courtroom made a motion to them. I myself observed this. I don't know if it was the same individual who was called to my attention the other day, but I feel that is an improper attempt to influence the jury."

"Can you point him out to me?" the judge asked.

"He has removed himself. I think Mrs. Hanna gave a note to the tipstaff to remove him."

"Do you know him to see him?"

"Yes."

"Do you know who he is?"

"He works for the city. I don't know his name."

Once the individual was identified, the judge retired the jury and summoned the spectator, a bear of a man with thick, dark hair. Judge McCracken determined that he made a thumbs-down signal to the jury and formerly worked for the city. "I advise you to get an attorney. We are going to have a hearing as soon as this trial is over.... You are instructed to stay off the courtroom premises."

Concerned with the possibility for a mistrial, Judge McCracken called Attorney Micacchione to the bench for a sidebar and asked, "What do you want by way of curative measures with respect to the jury at this time?"

"May I discuss this with my client, Your Honor?"

"Yes. We can question each juror individually in chambers, because we are willing to do the best to give Commonwealth and defendant a fair trial." All fourteen jurors admitted to seeing the gesture, but they agreed they could render a fair and impartial decision.

"Your Honor, I am satisfied with what was done," Micacchione stated.

"Put this on record. The court did not observe that, or we would have taken preventative measures immediately," the judge added.

"I understand, Your Honor. I do respectfully, even though there have been statements by every juror that this has not affected them, make a motion for a mistrial, because of the widespread nature of the situation and the gesture itself."

"What is your position, Mr. Williams?" the judge asked.

"I think the jurors' comments indicate it didn't affect them at all. In fact, they appeared to be insulted by the suggestion that it might affect them. I think the jurors have a strength of their own, and there is no basis for any motion."

"Well, I would put on record my observation of the way they reacted when they were asked about this. The court is satisfied they weren't influenced, and we will deny the motion for a mistrial. All right. It is 4:37. I believe you never did get a chance for redirect."

"Your Honor, may we approach the bench for a moment?" Micacchione lowered his voice and requested special precautions against television exposure since Channel 33 had recorded the guilty gesture. The judge agreed.

Micacchione continued with his redirect: "Mr. Atkinson, about the end of January, you were in the Lawrence County Jail, is that correct?"

"Yes."

"Was there a reason why you requested to be removed to some other facility?"

"Yes."

"What was the reason?"

"Dennis Alexander and John Thomas was arrested, and word got out I was supposed to have told Sergeant Abraham information." Atkinson spoke in a near whisper. An inveterate hypochondriac, he played his real and imagined ailments to the hilt.

"And they were arrested for what charge?"

"Homicide."

"No further questions." Micacchione picked up his pen and shifted in his seat.

Sergeant Abraham scanned the jury panel. The man in the fifth seat sat riveted to the witness. After hours of listening to testimony, the juror looked tired, drained by the tension of the trial.

Thursday morning opened with Micacchione's questioning of James Carungi, a dark, balding wiry police sergeant. "Was there some kind of relationship between these two?" The defense was referring to Lou Kadunce and Mary Akers. He stressed the word *relationship* to drive home the possibility of an affair as a motive to the jury. A female panel member leaned forward. Her body language confirmed the sexual impact of the interrogation.

"Yes."

Once Sergeant Carungi stepped down from the stand, the judge called for a sidebar. "Evidence Lou Kadunce was seeing another woman could be exculpatory to the defendant."

The D.A. countered, "Our evidence was he hadn't been seeing this girl for some time, and that relationship had terminated previous to the summer of 1978."

Micacchione clarified his thoughts on exculpatory evidence. "Your Honor, I know about an interview regarding what happened the night before on July 10 at school, showing the temper and demeanor of Larry Kadunce, based upon what the court now understands is the defense of this particular case." Abraham recollected Kadunce's feisty debate during his evening class on the importance of male dominance of the household.

"The defense is that Lou Kadunce killed his wife?" asked the judge.

"Absolutely."

"Of course, I don't know what the theory of the Commonwealth is, and that bears on whether or not it is exculpatory, that the defendant murdered these people because of a drug rip-off, or whether he is a hit man procured by Lawrence Kadunce to murder the wife because he wanted her out, and it does make a difference to what is exculpatory," Judge McCracken explained.

"We have put in evidence, Your Honor, that Mr. Kadunce is involved, that he furnished the key to this defendant," the D.A. expounded.

"Now, the defendant continues to try to inculcate Mr. Kadunce. The Commonwealth is attempting to exculpate him. I think, in the interest of justice and fair play, defense counsel should be given any and all evidence the Commonwealth has tending to inculcate Lawrence Kadunce or tending to exculpate the defendant, if you have anything of that nature," the judge ordered.

"All right," District Attorney Williams agreed.

The judge summarized his understanding of the defense and prosecution's assumptions regarding the case: "Both think Lawrence Kadunce is involved. Commonwealth theory is he procured these homicides through the defendant. Obviously, the defense's theory is Lawrence Kadunce perpetrated this by himself without any aid of the defendant. Is that correct?"

The opposing counsels agreed.

Attorney Micacchione called Captain William Carbone of the New Castle police, who eased to the stand and sat. Upon questioning, he described the route Lawrence Kadunce told him he took to work the day of the murders. "He first told me when he left home he had gone to the store next door to his place, got out of his car, looked in. The store was closed. He left, went through an alley over to Highland Avenue. He went south on Highland to a gas station, and it was closed. He continued south to North Street, turned right, went to Jefferson Street, turned south on Jefferson, down to the Public Square. He turned left, went up Washington Street to Croton, turned left on Croton to Crawford, turned right on Crawford and went to the home of Ron Silvis, and from there came back onto Croton, went to the gas station, got gas, went to Lawson's, got some pop and cigarettes, and from there came back down Croton to Fombelle's and from there he didn't recall how he had gotten to work."

"Now that was the statement he gave you at the scene of the crime, is that correct?"

"Yes."

"Did you conduct an investigation whether such a route was possible?"

"I didn't. I ordered Sergeant Carungi to investigate. I knew the south end of the Public Square was non-passible. The reconstruction of Washington Street was in progress, and he claimed he had turned at the south end of the square on Washington Street, and I distinctly recall him saying he remembered it because the American News Stand sits there."

"I see," Micacchione answered knowingly.

"So I had the officers check this, and we had found he had lied to us. There is no way he could have gotten through the Public Square, because the street was blocked." Kadunce changed his route the following day when he appeared with his attorney at the station.

Micacchione questioned the captain concerning Mr. Kadunce's attendance the night before the murders at a psychology class at New Castle Business College, where he left early.

"His instructor informed us that Mr. Kadunce, who seldom took part in any class discussion, took up practically the whole class in heavy argumentative situations with the instructor."

"What was the subject?"

"It dealt with unfaithful wives." Micacchione watched the courtroom heat up as the testimony tore into the husband's veracity and scored points for the defendant.

"Did he give you any other statements relative to what he did on July the tenth?"

"Several. On one occasion he told me he left Queens, had gone home, got his wife and daughter, they went shopping, and they went to some park, which he couldn't remember, and then on another occasion he said he and his wife had stayed home and watched television all night."

"So, again, you have different stories as to activities of that particular evening, is that correct?"

"Yes."

"Did he ever indicate to you what occurred on the morning of the murder prior to the time he left for work?"

"Yes, he told me at the scene that when he left for work that morning his wife was sitting on the edge of the bed and feeding the baby." Micacchione asked for "contrary information."

"On one occasion he told us when he left for work, his wife was laying in bed and feeding the baby....Another time he described that...his wife and the kids were still sleeping when he left the house....I think his final statement was his wife was lying in bed; the kids were sleeping, and he didn't want to kiss them goodbye because he had a cold and didn't want to spread it to them."

Following lunch recess, Micacchione asked to approach the bench to call a witness from Mount Pleasant out of order prior to cross.

Cynthia Collins, Mike Atkinson's sister, swore that her brother had been in Mount Pleasant on the day of the murders.

"Now, I ask you this, how are you able to affix these particular dates in your mind?"

"In 1978, it was the first birthday I celebrated with my father in a couple of years, and my husband's birthday is the twenty-sixth of June, and I baked a cake. I bought them presents, and that is how I remember."

"Are you sure this was 1978, as opposed to, let's say, 1979?"

"Yes, I'm positive, because in 1979, I had surgery that summer." She insists Mike departed on July 14, three days after the murder.

Cynthia Collins stepped down, and Captain Carbone returned to the stand. Attorney Micacchione asked, "Relative to Mr. Kadunce, did you ever as part of your investigation discover there were marital problems between him and Kathy Kadunce?"

"Mr. Kadunce was upset with the sexual activity between his wife and himself."

With sexual innuendo tantalizing the prurient interest of the jury, Micacchione pushed the attack on Kadunce's morality and the instability of the marriage.

"As a result of your investigation, were you ever advised by Mr. Kadunce that his wife and he were about to split?"

"No, not by Mr. Kadunce, but through…"

"Objection," challenged the D.A. "Hearsay!"

"Objection sustained," ruled Judge McCracken.

"Did Lou Kadunce ever relate circumstances whereby he felt Kathy was seeing another person?"

"Yes, he stated he believed Kathy was having an affair, and that is why she was always going downtown."

"Were you advised by Mr. Silvis that Mr. Kadunce owned any type of weapons in his home?"

"Yes, Mr. Silvis stated he owned a .22 pistol."

"Captain, I am going to show you what has been listed as Commonwealth's Exhibit 10 and ask if you can identify that?"

"Yes, this is the cigarette butt found on the floor in the bathroom near the head of the victim."

"Did you have an opportunity to examine that butt at the time it was discovered?"

"Yes."

"What did you find as a result of making comparisons?"

"That it was the same type as in the ashtrays in the living room and the kitchen."

"All right. Did you make any other comparisons between this particular butt and the brand of cigarettes Larry Kadunce smoked at the time?"

"Yes, I did. The cigarettes Larry Kadunce smoked seemed to be the same type that this butt would be from."

D.A. Williams cross-examined: "Do you know what kind of cigarette it is?"

"No, I don't."

"Do you know what kind Larry smoked?"

"No, I don't."

"Did you ask him what kind he smoked?"

Captain Carbone cringed. The investigation had been sloppy, and he knew it. "I…no…I didn't ask Larry directly what kind of cigarette he smoked."

"Well then, how can you say that is the kind he smoked?"

Carbone tried to cover his tracks. "Because it was similar to the type Larry smoked. He lit several in my company."

"And do you know whether he always smoked the same brand?"

"No, I don't." Carbone wilted before the D.A.'s assault, reducing his value to the defense.

Williams passed the witness to Micacchione, who asked for a description of Kadunce's sexual problems.

"Lou stated he was not able to ejaculate to a conclusion."

"Did he express what Kathy was doing as a result of this?"

"He stated he thought she was seeing another man."

"Did he state whether he had seen his wife with another person?"

"No, he didn't."

"Did he ever state to you he suspected anyone of being that person?"

"Yes." The witness checked his notes to refresh his memory. "Lamont Polding."

"Did Lou Kadunce ever express that Kathy thought he was seeing someone else?"

"Yes," Lou mentioned Kathy had accused him of seeing someone at work.

"Did Mr. Silvis ever express that he made a pass at Kathy?"

"Yes."

"Did Mr. Silvis indicate Lou Kadunce was aware of this?"

"Mr. Silvis did not indicate Mr. Kadunce was aware of it."

"No further questions." Micacchione returned to the seat beside his client, who leaned toward his lawyer and whispered: "How're we doing?"

"As well as can be expected." Micacchione patted his client's shoulder.

During cross-examination, the D.A. asked the police captain if animosity existed between him and Lou Kadunce.

Carbone answered without hesitation. "Lou becomes upset in my presence at any time and any place."

During redirect, Micacchione brought up the tension between Kathy's father, Richard Buckel, and Lou following the murders.

"Were words passed between Mr. Buckel and Mr. Kadunce?"

"Yes."

"Did Mr. Kadunce make a statement that Mr. Buckel had better stop pushing him the way Kathy did?"

"Yes."

Having highlighted the explosive pressure damaging the marriage, Micacchione allowed the court to excuse the witness. "Call your next witness," the judge instructed.

"Defense rests."

"Any rebuttal, Mr. Williams?"

"We do, Your Honor. We call Kathy Laux."

The twenty-nine-year-old niece of Frank Costal entered the courtroom and was sworn in.

"Do you know Michael Atkinson?"

"Yes."

"Have you ever dated him?"

"No."

"Have you ever had any drug dealings with him?"

"No."

"Do you have a daughter named Dawn?"

"No." Atkinson had stipulated in court that Kathy Laux had a daughter named Dawn, the same age as the deceased Dawn Kadunce.

"Did you ever?"

"No." Mike had been caught in another lie. He shrugged his shoulders and lowered his eyes to avoid the stares of the jurors. Micacchione's frown reflected the damage done by the witness's testimony. As Kathy Laux departed and Atkinson followed her with his eyes, Abraham chalked up another point for the good guys on his pad.

Attorney Williams called William Brothers, a nineteen-year-old tough, to the stand. Micacchione objected on the grounds of relevancy and procedure, but Judge McCracken overruled.

"Mike told me the lady's husband was a homosexual. He wanted his wife to leave home, and she didn't want to leave. Mike had gotten a key, and he told me he killed the lady, and Frank killed the baby," the witness related.

Micacchione examined him closely, "Mr. Brothers what are you in jail for?"

"Burglary, robbery, conspiracy."

"Did you make a deal?"

"No, sir, I did not."

"Has your attorney been discussing this with the district attorney?"

"No, he was present at the time I was talking to my attorney, but we didn't make no deal."

Frank O'Neill followed William Brothers to the witness stand. The D.A. opened, "Did you have a conversation with Mr. Atkinson during the month of July?"

"Yes. He just asked me if I would testify that I seen him sell the gun to Mr. Savage in 1976."

"And did you see him sell a gun to Mr. Savage?"

"No, not eye to eye, but Mr. Savage did have the gun."

"What did Mr. Atkinson say to your not having any knowledge of his selling the gun?"

"He wanted to know if I would testify that I seen him sell the gun to Savage."

"Well, did you agree to that?"

"I first did, and I said no later on."

"Did he ask you to testify to any other matter?"

"He didn't ask me to say it, but he told me he was out of Pennsylvania in 1978." Williams turned the witness over to the defense.

Micacchione brought out the fact that O'Neill's wife, Linda, had dated Mike before their marriage and also afterward. Mike relished the witness's discomfort and embarrassment. Like the proverbial cat who devoured a canary, the defendant gloried in the moment, oblivious to the future peril that might befall him. Micacchione returned to his desk after alluding to possible intimacy between O'Neill's wife and Atkinson. Abraham tried not to smile. For an ugly dude, Mike Atkinson apparently had a way with the ladies.

The following morning, October 3, Judge McCracken met with the defense attorney, the district attorney and his client in private regarding Micacchione's suspension. After the agreement of all parties, Judge McCracken agreed to contact the Pennsylvania Supreme Court to allow an extension under Rule 217, whereby the presiding judge can protect the rights of a client and allow the practice of a formerly admitted attorney.

With the matter of Micacchione's participation resolved, the D.A. recalled Darlene Pounds, who reaffirmed she had been in Mount Pleasant in June 1978 rather than July 1978, as Atkinson claimed.

Testimony closed at 10:35 a.m. following the questioning of Darlene Pounds. Mike leaned over to his attorney and asked, "Counselor, how does it look?"

"Mike, I think we've got a shot, but we'll just have to wait and see," Micacchione reassured his client.

The court recessed the jury, which remained sequestered over the weekend in preparation for final arguments at 9:00 a.m. on Monday, October 6. Micacchione objected to several photographs scheduled for the jury's consideration as overly inflammatory. Judge McCracken eliminated Exhibit 100, a gruesome photograph of Dawn Kadunce on a table in the morgue. Discussions on evidence and procedures lasted until four o'clock in the afternoon.

The judge ordered the courtroom doors to be locked. For two and a half hours, the opposing attorneys presented their closing arguments. Micacchione admitted his client was a storyteller, but not a murderer. His booming voice could be heard all the way down the hallway as he waved his arms from side to side and accused the husband of murder.

After lunch, the judge began his charge, instructing the jury on the law: "The defendant has been charged on Bill of Indictment Number 192 of 1980 with murder in the first degree, charging the defendant did commit a criminal homicide by intentionally and knowingly causing the death of Kathy Kadunce, that he did feloniously, willfully, and of malice forethought, kill and murder the said Kathy Kadunce by a criminal act. The same bill of indictment charges murder in the third degree. The defendant also was charged on a Bill of Indictment Number 192A for murder of the first and second degree of Dawn Kadunce."

Judge McCracken explained the state had the responsibility to prove beyond a reasonable doubt the defendant caused a death intentionally, deliberately and with premeditation in order to find the defendant guilty of first-degree murder. He informed the jury of the penalties, life imprisonment for murder in the first degree and a maximum sentence of twenty years and a fine of up to $25,000 for a conviction of murder in the third degree.

The judge admonished the jury,

> *A fundamental principle of our system of criminal law is the defendant is presumed to be innocent....The Commonwealth has the burden of proving each and every element of the crime charged, and the defendant is guilty beyond a reasonable doubt.*
>
> *The law requires the court to review testimony with you....If you conclude one of the witnesses testified falsely, you may disregard everything the witness said. However, you are not required to disregard everything. It is entirely possible the witness testified falsely in one respect, but truthfully about everything else. If that is the situation, you may accept that part of his testimony which is truth and reject that part which is false.*

For nearly two hours, the judge reviewed the evidence of the case provided by fifty-five witnesses, making every effort to present impartially the testimony of each witness. "Upon retiring to deliberate, you should select one of you to be the foreman or forelady. He or she will announce the verdict. When you reach a verdict, you will advise the tipstaff, who will be stationed immediately outside of your room....The verdict must be unanimous. That means each of you must agree to it."

Following eleven days of testimony, the tipstaff provided the panel with the evidence exhibits along with verdict slips. After only four hours, the jury reached a verdict and court reconvened.

"To the spectators in the audience, there will be absolutely no reaction sequential to the verdict," the judge cautioned.

This might be George Micacchione's last case for several years, possibly his last case ever. He had given it his all. Ego urged him to look for an acquittal, although the odds favored a guilty verdict.

The prothonotary read: "In the case of Commonwealth versus Mike Atkinson, Criminal Action Number 192 of 1980, Kathy Kadunce, we the jurors find the defendant, Mike Atkinson, on the charge of murder in the first degree guilty. And in the case of Commonwealth versus Mike Atkinson, Criminal Action 192A of 1980, Dawn Kadunce, we the jurors find the defendant, Mike Atkinson, on the charge of murder in the first degree not guilty. On the charge of murder in the third degree guilty."

"If this is your verdict, do you all agree?" asked the judge

"Yes," the jury foreman responded. The judge polled the panel individually at George Micacchione's request.

"Mr. Atkinson, if you feel you have not been given a fair trial, or I made a mistake in any of my rulings on the law, you have the right to file a motion setting forth any complaints within ten days of this date. You have the right to have the assistance of an attorney in preparing the motion. If you don't have an attorney and cannot afford one, one will be provided by court to represent you free of charge. Do you understand that, sir?"

"Yes," Atkinson answered without a trace of emotion.

"Either counsel have anything for the record?"

"We move the commitment of the defendant, Your Honor," stated the D.A.

"Nothing," responded Micacchione, his spirit battered but unbroken.

With the trial over, Gig greeted Chuck and extended a hand for a congratulatory shake. "Well, Babe, great job. One down, two to go." Interestingly, Queen's hit song "Another One Bites the Dust" was leading the pop charts.

"Costal next," Chuck shot back with a thumbs-up sign.

"See you at Medure's at seven. We're going to do some big time celebrating tonight," Gig answered with a devilish glint in his eye.

11

THE COSTAL TRIAL

The trial of Frank Costal opened on a freezing Monday, January 12, 1981, with former prosecuting attorney and no-nonsense judge the Honorable William R. Balph presiding. The thermometer had sunk to six degrees below zero. On the national front, the soap opera *Dynasty* began a nine-year run on television that evening, and a militant group in Puerto Rico blew up nine air national guard jet fighter planes.

In New Castle, Robert T. Barletta and Harry O. Falls faced the daunting task of defending Frank Costal. District Attorney Don Williams, the prosecutor at the Atkinson trial, represented the Commonwealth. The judge implemented strong security for this high-profile trial. A constable guarded the third floor, and a plainclothes officer covered the second.

The defendant's craggy face, front-and-center homosexuality, Satanism, coterie of misfit friends and carnival background compounded with a conservative rural jury from nearby Crawford County to present nearly impossible hurdles for Barletta and Falls.

Attorney Frank Verterano, who represented Atkinson in the Rosie Puz murder trial, approached the district attorney with an offer for his client to testify on behalf of the Commonwealth in exchange for leniency. The D.A. sent Sergeant Abraham and Lieutenant Gagliardo to the Beaver County Jail to iron out the pre-trial details.

"Mike, did you mean it when you said you hated me while you were on the stand?" Chuck asked, pulling the prisoner's chain.

"Naw, I didn't mean nothing by it," the words oozed from Mike's lips.

Left: Judge William Balph. *Lawrence County Bar Association.*

Right: Attorney Robert Barletta. *Lawrence County Bar Association.*

"How are you getting on?" Gig asked.

"It's bad here, and I'm bored. A radio would help pass the time."

"Maybe we can help if you play ball with us." Mike seemed to agree.

As the two cops left the jail, Gig nudged Chuck. "Babe, how come I always feel like I need a shower after time with Mike?"

"He does make your skin crawl, but he's going to bring us Costal, and that's what counts."

Gig and Chuck stopped at Jamesway Discount and bought a seven-dollar transistor radio. When they returned to the jail and handed it to Mike, his face lit up like a birthday boy getting his first bike. He became cooperative and promised to give up Costal in return for some dental work, immunity from the death penalty in the Puz case and a dismissal of charges against his father. Chuck bought him a powder-blue jacket, coordinating slacks, a dress shirt and a tie at the Salvation Army secondhand store to wear when he testified to make him look respectable.

Costal's attorneys had little hope for an acquittal but provided the strongest defense they could muster. To make a better impression on the jury, Costal trimmed his long hair and shaved his beard. Although he still projected a

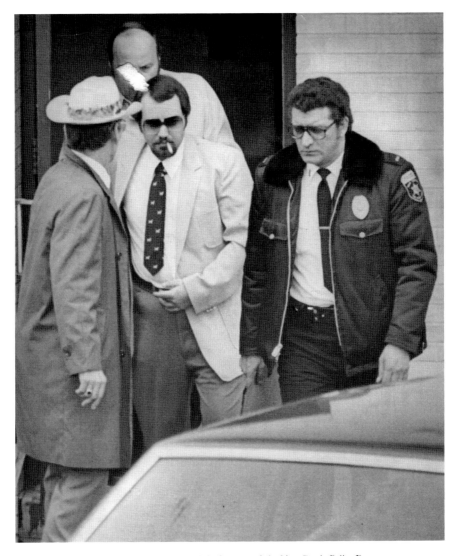

Atkinson after testifying at the Costal trial. *Courtesy of the New Castle Police Department.*

seedy look, he appeared more than presentable in a dark navy suit and tie. Throughout the trial, Frank stared blankly at the table in front of him, rarely looking at the jury, the witnesses or the district attorney.

Whenever the crush of the courtroom squeezed him like a boa constrictor, stealing the breath from his lungs, Costal's eyes glazed over as he disassociated himself from his body. Then, employing his gift of transmigration, he

Frank Costal leaving court. *Courtesy of the New Castle Police Department.*

psyched up his spirit to soar from his present captivity and floated into the distant world of circus clowns, trapeze artists and lion tamers.

"Ladies and gentlemen, it's a privilege to make an opening statement…to give you a picture of what is coming," the D.A.'s voice resonated with the strength of an avenging angel about to strike the snake slithering through the Garden of Eden, an anathema to his religious convictions. "You will hear testimony from people who have beheld the lifestyle of Mr. Costal, how he lived on Highland Avenue, that he had a homosexual existence, that he stayed with several people. They will discuss his habits of being a satanic priest, how he had influence over the people he stayed with. One of the persons was Michael Atkinson. The evidence will show Michael Atkinson was his boyfriend in a sexual relationship, that he had accouterments of this satanic cult, which influenced people to listen to him. You will hear testimony as to the demeanor of Mr. Costal when he was asked about this offense. After hearing this testimony we'll ask you to conclude he was a participant in the deaths of Kathy and Dawn Kadunce, and we'll ask you to convict him of murder."

At the end of the opening statement, Barletta called for a sidebar. "Your Honor, we object to portions of the Commonwealth's opening statement and request the court declare a mistrial due to the prejudicial nature of these statements, especially his references to the defendant as a homosexual and…as a satanic priest who influences other people." Judge Balph refused the motion.

"Your Honor, we would also place a motion for mistrial on references made by the district attorney including Mike Atkinson and his connection with that person."

"Mr. Williams?" asked the court.

"We'll present evidence Mike Atkinson did homosexual acts, and he was the person Mr. Costal went with to that house."

"Your Honor, the Commonwealth is intending to try this case using guilt by association.…Mr. Atkinson is not on trial here. The only question is the

District Attorney Don Williams addresses the jury. *Courtesy of the New Castle Police Department.*

Judge William Balph and Attorney Barletta. *Courtesy of the New Castle Police Department.*

guilt or innocence of Mr. Costal." The court again refused Barletta's motion for a mistrial.

Barletta faced huge odds against Costal's acquittal. The combination of a Bible-thumping district attorney, unfavorable judge rulings and a flawed client added to the growing list of handicaps. Barletta, a competent Notre Dame–educated lawyer, and his co-attorney Harry Falls were paddling upstream in a leaky boat.

A handful of witnesses from the Atkinson trial reappeared in that of Costal's. In addition, dozens of new ones came to the forefront to reinforce Costal's homosexuality and witchcraft. Graphic photographs of Costal's apartment validated the theory of cult to the jury, much to the dismay of the defense attorneys.

The D.A. explained his theory about Costal in a sidebar, and the judge bought it: "He utilized his prowess as a satanic priest to get people under his control so he could get them to do things he wanted done for his sadistic ends. He brought Atkinson into that program, and our evidence shows that Atkinson was with him, and they did this crime, and they did it in a way representative of satanic belief." How could the jury not draw a parallel between the brutality of the Kadunce killings and the helter-skelter violence committed by Charles Manson's followers less than a decade earlier in California?

"Your Honor, we would place a continuing objection to further testimony concerning Satanism, witchcraft and devil worship. The defense is also making a continuing objection against any testimony on homosexuality," Barletta stated for the record.

Witness George Koziol described Costal's ability to put "curses on people using black candles. He would set them up and light them and sit in the middle of the floor with his legs crossed and start speaking some strange language." Koziol once observed Frank and Mike in their undershorts kissing each other.

Officer John Robertson described the discovery of hair from a dog found in Dawn's bedroom. Although the fur appeared similar to that of a German Shepherd, Robertson could not swear it came from Dudoic's dog, Schultz.

Twenty-one-year-old ninth-grade dropout Steve Hammond, a former lover of Frank's, described the defendant's power to control people. Frank terrified the youth when he warned him that he intended to teleport his spirit and follow him home.

"Did he ever furnish you drugs, Steve?" asked the D.A.

"I smoked pot up there."

"Were you afraid of him?"

"Yes, he can put curses on people."

Attorney Falls objected, "Your Honor, I think this witness's testimony is a gratuitous attempt to show homosexuality and inflame the jury, not to show any connection with the case for which Mr. Costal is being tried."

"Your Honor," countered the D.A. "This witness shows the exercise of power over people, mainly over people that were slow or retarded. We intend to put into evidence that Mike Atkinson was that kind of person, too." The court denied Falls's motion to strike.

Another ex-boyfriend, slow-speaking, thirty-year-old, ex-con Paul Weiblinger, testified that when Frank caught him playing cards with a woman, he called her filthy names and threatened to curse her. The next morning, in a fit of jealousy, Frank attempted to stab him with a sword.

Eighteen-year-old Kevin Delaney described the ritual for a human sacrifice as explained to him by Costal, which included laying them on a rug after drugging them and stabbing the victim seventeen times.

"Did he ever see this done?" asked the D.A.

"He witnessed it once, but he wouldn't tell me where and when."

"How did he look?"

"Wild hair and beard. He scared the hell out of me."

"Have you seen him recently during the court proceedings?"

"Yes, I have. He looks like a lawyer now." A titter of laughter ran through the courtroom. The judge, stifling his own urge, rapped his gavel for quiet.

"The prosecution calls Jeffrey Wade." The fifteen-year-old cherub appeared on the stand. He testified to visiting with Costal while sitting on a bench at the Towne Mall in November 1978.

"Did you ever ask him if he knew anything about the Kadunce case?"

"Yes, I just come straight out and asked him."

"What did he tell you, Jeff?"

"He told me he was there. He did not help Atkinson murder her. They were never even going to that house. The husband was supposed to know something about some dope, and instead they went into the house. Frank was with Atkinson, but he wasn't in on the murder."

"Did he say whether or not he saw it?"

"He said Atkinson was giving Mrs. Kadunce a hard time, slapping her around and hitting her, trying to convince her about some kind of dope. She wouldn't say anything, so they grabbed the child. It wasn't they; it was Atkinson, and started hitting the child to persuade Mrs. Kadunce to tell them."

"And what happened after that?"

"It didn't seem to be doing any good, so Atkinson started hitting the kid more. So, he got carried away, and Atkinson started beating the mother with the knife, and the child. First they got the child."

"Why did he say he did this thing?"

"He stood and watched. He didn't do nothing." The witness looked toward the defendant's chair but quickly glanced away toward the floor.

Sergeant Abraham, the prosecuting officer for the police, sat, listened and weighed the facts. Jeffrey Wade had spun a great story, so good he probably believed every word of it. However, the evidence showed the mother and daughter died without much of a struggle. In fact, Dawn probably died in her bed. Had Jeffrey embellished what Frank may or may not have said?

"Did he say anything about what the police thought?" the D.A. continued.

"That Mr. Kadunce was supposed to be a little bit mental, because he was in Vietnam. They thought he did it."

The Commonwealth next summoned fifty-year-old surgical nurse Jane Garcia, a self-proclaimed psychologist and a minister in the Pentecostal Church, who believed Frank may have been involved in the unsolved shooting of four-year-old Melanie Gargasz and her thirty-seven-year-old babysitter Beverly Withers, killed in 1975. Mrs. Garcia testified to seeing Costal and Kadunce together on several occasions in 1978. She specifically mentioned seeing Frank clad in red bikini underwear and silk hose with Larry at the Highland Avenue apartment.

Jane met Costal through her daughter Susan, who suffered a stroke and was partially paralyzed on her left side. Frank told Susan he could cure her by immersing her nude body in a bathtub filled with salts. He offered to wrap her in a white robe and position her on a special carpet. If he mouthed the proper incantation, she would be healed. When Susan confided in her mother, Jane asked to meet this so-called wizard, who became her friend and "controller." He took Jane to the grave of the local nineteenth-century witch Mary Black and later loaned her books on Satanism and witchcraft. Frank told her he could do away with her husband for twenty-five dollars if he mistreated her. He showed her a black pin and a white pin and said if she obtained a lock of the victim's hair, he could do away with him by burning a black candle and sticking the pins in it. Jane believed Frank, a high priest in the Sybileek Satanist Organization, possessed the power to punish those who opposed him.

When the hospital admitted Frank for heart problems, he called Jane to get him some Pall Malls. Jane gave the excuse that she had no car at the moment. Frank told her he knew she had three cars available. Frank might have known she owned two cars, but her husband had purchased a third that very day.

Since Jane did not drive, she had her youngest daughter drive her to the store for the cigarettes. After giving them to Frank, they returned to the new car and tried to start it. When the car stalled, Jane and her daughter marched back to Frank's room and demanded to know what he had done. Frank told her to return to the car and try again. The car started immediately.

Frank hung plastic bats in his apartment to represent his followers. One day, Susan grew ill and found herself in the hospital. Within the hour, Frank mysteriously appeared in her room. When Susan asked how he knew she was there, he answered, "Because your bat has fallen from the ceiling." Frank gave Susan a bloodstone pendant and told her to wear it until it turned red. Then, she should remove it since the impurities from her body would be gone.

Jane recalled Frank confessing to shooting Kathy Kadunce over a drug deal gone awry. Frank told her Atkinson and the husband also had been involved.

The prosecution ended the day by introducing *The Witches Bible*, a satanic book Frank had loaned Jane inscribed with the names "Frank Batzel and L. Kadunce." Frank frequently used his stepfather's name, Batzel, rather than Costal.

Judy Antoniotti testified that Frank told her, "Your husband is my husband." She drew a smile from Costal and a laugh from the audience when she described the defendant's description of his monthly disability check as "mother's assistance."

Twenty-seven-year-old Cleveland native David Jackson, a former inmate in the Lawrence County Jail, testified to serving time as Costal's cellmate. Jackson recalled Costal, after awakening at three o'clock in the morning, approaching his bunk. "He was crying, and he woke me up. He called me by name. I was half-asleep, but I heard every word he told me. He said he couldn't live with himself, that he was sorry he did it. And I asked, 'Did what?' That him and Mike Atkinson had stabbed this lady and child to death, and he never knew what came over him to make him do it."

"Did he ever make any explanation of why he did it?"

"The later part of July he stated he wasn't heavy with Mike Atkinson. He knows Mike Atkinson had committed the murders.…He said he didn't know what came over him. He didn't mean to do it."

Jackson also remembered Costal watching a television show about battered children. "I happened to raise up on my bunk, and the television was showing how a child was beaten and burned with cigarettes, and Mr. Costal was laughing. I didn't think it was funny."

"Did you have words with him?"

"I told him, 'You're sick, you're a crazy man, you're…'"

"Your Honor, I object to the witness's words and request they be stricken," cut in Barletta.

"Sustained," ruled the judge. "Ladies and gentlemen of the jury, disregard what the witness said to Mr. Costal."

Each day, the *New Castle News* reported the previous day's testimony on its front page, generating a local reading frenzy. People on the streets tossed out their own recollections of the Witch of Highland Avenue, a frequent downtown walker. Residents lined up outside the courtroom more than an hour in advance of the trial for a shot at one of the sixty spectator seats, anxious to suck in the excitement of sex, murder and Satanism without resorting to television shows like Phil Donahue's. With a no-reserved seating policy, late arrivers like Costal's mother, Mrs. Tony Figaro, and Kathy Kadunce's father, Richard Buckel, found themselves shut out from the Thursday, January 15 session.

Witness Marshall Dillon claimed that Costal "knew Mrs. Kadunce and used to go up there."

Mike Atkinson, dressed in a tie and jacket, lumbered to the stand. His face looked drawn, but his shark eyes maintained their icy intensity. Sergeant Abraham, sitting beside the district attorney, wondered what outlandish stories Mike would fabricate for the jury. D.A. Williams rose to question Mike.

"Do you know the defendant, Frank Costal?"

"Yes, I do."

"Did you associate with him in 1978?"

"Yes, I did."

"Did you know Kathy Kadunce?"

"Yes, I did."

"Where did you first meet her?"

"Towne Mall. I met her through Frank Costal."

"Back in '77, did you meet her more than one time that year?"

"Yes, I'd say nine times."

"Was Costal with you any of those times?"

"Twice at his apartment, at the mall and Eat 'n Park on Washington Street."

"Did you meet with her in 1978?"

"Yes."

"Did you know she was married?"

"Not in '77."

"When did you find out?"

"About three weeks before she had the baby."

"Do you have idea when that was?"

"If I'm not mistaken, it was in May or April of 1978."

"Where did you meet her on that occasion?"

"At the mall."

"Who was with you?"

"I was by myself. I walked in. I seen Frank, and that's when I ran into Kathy."

"Was it in one of the restaurants?"

"Murphy's Coffee Shop.…That's when I found that Kathy was married."

"After this time you met Kathy and Larry at the mall, when was the next time you saw her?"

Mike paused and scratched his head. "July 11."

"Where?"

"Their house."

"Tell us about your meeting with Larry on July 10?…Who else was there when you met him?"

"Frank Costal, John…not Dudash…I can't pronounce his last name."

"Is it Dudoic?"

"Dudoic. Yes, sir."

"The three of you?"

"Four."

"Who was the other?"

"Larry Kadunce."

"And where did the meeting take place?"

"I believe it's the Burger King."

"What time of day did you meet at Burger King?"

"John and I was out fishing and came back around seven o'clock."

"Was Frank there?"

"Frank and Larry was sitting at the Burger Chef."

"Did you stay there a while together, all four of you?"

"About forty minutes."

"Did you have a conversation with Frank there?"

"Yes, over how much a hundred hits of speed and Percodans are?"

"Why was Frank interested in that?"

"I paid Frank $60 for the speed and $45 for the Percodans."

"When had you given that to him?"

"About three days before that."

"Why did he bring up the conversation?"

"He said Larry's wife found the pills and supposedly flushed them down the toilet."

"Was there further discussion about that?"

"We was supposed to meet the next morning."

"Who was?"

"Frank and I and Larry Kadunce and John Dudoic…at Frank's apartment."

"Why was Frank interested in meeting the next day?"

"Because I was blaming him for getting ripped off for my money."

"Did you ask where the stuff was?"

"Yes. He said he was getting it off of Larry Kadunce."

"What time did the meeting break up?"

"I'd say about twenty minutes to eight." Abraham thought about the timing. He recalled that Kadunce had been in class at New Castle Business College around this time. Mike was a switcher. Throughout the investigation, he changed names, dates and times to suit his needs, frequently contradicting his own testimony from one interview to the next.

Mike explained that he and John Dudoic went fishing at Medusa Lake after leaving Frank the evening prior to the murders. The two drank beers and smoked pot until five o'clock in the morning.

"Was it still dark?"

"I believe so. I couldn't see too straight." Mike grinned at his attempt to inject humor.

"Then what did you do?"

"We left and came back to New Castle, drove up to Frank's. I knocked on the door; he answered. I asked him if he wanted any fish, and he said, 'No.' So, John and I left and came back down to the Southside to a man that lives on the corner, and I gave him some fish."

"Who was that?"

"John Dickson." Abraham recalled that Dickson remembered getting the fish but was hazy on the date. From Dickson's, Atkinson and Dudoic drove back to Costal's apartment.

"When you arrived at Frank's, what was he doing?" the D.A. asked.

"Him and Larry Kadunce was getting out of bed."

"They were undressed when you got there?"

"Yes."

"Was there any reason for going to Kathy's house?"

"I was looking for one hundred hits of Black Beauties and fifty hits of Percodan. I paid Frank for them, and he was supposed to give Larry the money for them."

"How did you leave?"

"In John's car."

"Who was driving?"

"I was."

"Where was John?"

"John was in the front seat with me. Larry and Frank was in the back seat. Schultz, John's German Shepherd, was jumping from the front to the backseat."

"Why were you driving?"

"John wasn't in too good of a condition."

"He'd been drinking, too?"

"Drinking and smoking."

Mike parked beside Fast 'n Friendly.

"We got out of the car, closed the doors, walked up North Jefferson through the backyard of Larry Kadunce's house."

The four men entered the house according to the witness. The door was unlocked. Mike walked into the kitchen and boiled water for coffee. He lit a cigarette. After a few minutes, he heard the sound of running water coming from upstairs.

"Did you hear anything else?"

"I heard a female voice....She popped up and said, 'I see you got your faggot boyfriends with you.'" A gasp emanated from the gallery. The judge lowered his gavel to hush the disruption.

"Was there more than one voice?"

"There was Larry's voice running back and forth."

"What else did you hear?"

"I heard a child's voice. She said, 'Daddy, I have to go to the bathroom.'"

"Did you hear anything in response?"

"Larry Kadunce said, 'God damn, wait awhile, not right now.' Then, Larry called me upstairs."

"I turned around and walked up the stairs." Mike handed the cup of coffee he carried in his right hand to John. "Larry called again. I said, 'Where are you?' He said, 'The bathroom.'" Mike entered the bathroom to the shouts of the couple arguing. He sat on the side of the tub.

"What did Larry have on then?"

"He had blue coveralls and a pair of sandals."

"What did Kathy have on?"

"She was in the nude."

"Why did you sit down?"

"I couldn't stand too good." The previous night's beers and grass had taken their toll.

"What went on while you were sitting there?"

"Well, I popped up and asked Kathy, 'Did you find two bottles of pills?' She stated, 'No.'"

"Did you have a cigarette with you, Mike?"

"Yes, I did."

"What did you do with it?"

"I put the cigarette out in the bathtub."

Sergeant Abraham conjectured why the police hadn't spent more time analyzing the cigarette butts found in the bathroom the day of the murder. They had been so certain the husband had done the killings that they overlooked evidence.

According to Mike, Kadunce asked him if he was having an affair with his wife. Mike denied it, but Kathy supposedly snarled at her husband, "Neither one of the kids belong to you. It's a toss up between your nephew and Mike."

"What did you do next?"

"I got teed off. I stood up and hit her beside the head and walked out of the room." A female juror shifted her eyes away from the witness.

"What did you hit her with?"

"At that time, I had a full can of beer in my hand." Abraham remembered the autopsy showed no signs of a struggle of any kind.

"Where did you go?"

"I went downstairs."

"What happened then?"

"I heard Kathy screaming, and then she yelled, 'Quit pulling my hair.' And she screamed again, 'Why did you kick me there?' John asked me what was going on."

"Where was John?"

"At the bottom of the steps."

"Then what?"

"It sounded like a firecracker going off."

"How loud?"

"Not really loud, loud enough you could hear it through the house,"

"What did you do then?"

"John was the first one at the top of the steps. By the time I got there, because I tripped over the dog going up, I got to the bathroom and asked Larry what was going on?"

Atkinson captured the courtroom's full attention as he wove a story of drugs, adultery and murder.

"What did he look like?"

"He was standing there and holding a pistol in his hand." Jane Garcia advised Abraham that Costal claimed to have shot Kathy. He would have to sort out these details at a later date.

"What kind of pistol?" the D.A. continued.

"It was a revolver. I'd say between a four-to-six-inch barrel. The type of gun it was, I couldn't say."

"Did you look in the bathroom then?"

"I went through the door, looked around. Kathy was on her knees with her hand holding her stomach and her head laying on the floor."

"Did you see Frank anywhere?"

"Not at that time. I was standing there talking to Larry, trying to find out what the hell was going on. That's when Frank came out of the room. I believe it was the first room on the left as you're going up the stairs."

"What did Frank do?"

"He pushed me out of the way. I looked at my shirt, and I had a handprint of blood on it."

The room grew eerily quiet—not a word, not a sound could be heard as the D.A. paused to allow the shock waves of Atkinson's words to grow in seismic magnitude.

"What did you do then?"

"I went downstairs. Larry was already there. I asked him what was going on; he wouldn't answer. John came down, the dog following him. I said, 'Let's go,' and we left."

Atkinson testified that he and John drove downtown while Larry and Frank walked across Wilmington Road. When he reached downtown, he turned to John, who was driving, and said, "You know, our fingerprints are in that house." John returned to the house for fifteen or twenty minutes to clean up while Mike sat in the car with the dog.

"Have any problems with the dog?"

"Yes, when John left the car, Schultz tried to jump out. I grabbed him, and he snapped at me."

Dudoic returned and handed Mike his cigarettes and a lighter. He also gave Mike a bloody butcher knife wrapped in a scrap of denim fabric. John asked Mike to put the weapon in a fishing box on the back seat of the car.

"How'd John look when he came out of there?"

"Sick, he threw up over the back seat. He told me to drive, because he was too sick." Mike said he ran a red light while hurrying home to burn the bloody T-shirt he had worn at the Kadunce's.

"I made some coffee. I couldn't drink it. I drank a fifth of Bush. I had it in the refrigerator. John and I left from there to Frank's."

The time was approximately 9:30 in the morning. Frank had changed back into his red bikini underwear and was tripping on a combination of acid and his pulsating psych lights. He told Mike, "The bats were flying."

John asked Frank what happened, but Frank ignored the question. John smacked him on the side of his head with his open hand. Sergeant Abraham took in the testimony with a big dose of doubt. He believed Dudoic lacked the spine to strike Costal. Mike the "switcher," again was changing characters and stories to fit his needs. Only Mike would have the guts to slap Costal.

John took the knife from the tackle box and asked Frank what he wanted done with it.

"What did Frank say?" the D.A. asked.

"He kept saying, 'The bats is flying. Give it to Mike, and he'll get rid of it where he goes fishing.'"

After leaving Frank's, Mike picked up some beer at his house. Back in the car, John, who was driving, sporting disheveled shoulder-length hair and a Van Gogh beard, removed a bottle holding one hundred hits of Black Beauties from his pocket and silently handed it to Mike.

"Did he show you any other bottles?"

"He showed me a bottle that had fifty Percodans in it."

Later in the day, Mike returned to Medusa Lake to fish, where he heaved the knife into the middle of the water. He claimed to have gone to St. Francis Hospital on the twelfth for four stitches in his hand.

"For what?" asks the D.A.

"From where the dog bit me." Atkinson showed the scar to the jury and explained Schultz had bit him while he waited in the car in the driveway at the Kadunce house. Hospital records indicated Atkinson visited the hospital the month prior rather than July 12.

Mike testified that his father drove him to his sister's house in Mount Pleasant the evening of the twelfth until the sixteenth.

"Did you see Larry anymore?"

"Not until '79."

"Where did you see him then?"

"The first week of December '79, I was staying in Ellwood at the time. I borrowed a friend's car and went to Frank's to see about getting some weed. Frank and Larry was sitting there. That's when I first heard John committed suicide." John Dudoic took his own life on November 15, 1979.

"Were you frightened any?"

"That day, yes. Larry Kadunce stuck a gun in my face after he came down from his wife and stated if I ever testified, they know where my two children are, they know where my mother is and they know about my father. The same thing was stated to me the first week of December 1979." Mike left and said he never visited Frank's apartment again. The next time he saw Costal was in the Lawrence County Jail in March 1980.

"Did you ever know Frank Costal as the high priest?"

"Yes, he used to wear a high priest's gown. He had an altar at his house. He had rubber bats hanging from his chandelier. He had two parrots. He kept saying they was vultures. He used to have a Venus fly trap. He used to give it raw blood from his hand to make it grow."

When Atkinson attempted to describe a Costal suicide attempt, Judge Balph cautioned him to answer only the questions asked.

During cross-examination, Robert Barletta attacked the truthfulness of the witness. The defense portrayed Mike Atkinson as a convicted rapist accused of murdering Rosie Puz, an old woman who lived in his building. Barletta questioned the witness about a special deal to reduce other charges in exchange for incriminating Costal. Although Atkinson denied any such arrangement, his answers betrayed fabrications and half-truths. One by one, the defense reviewed Atkinson's false statements, allowing each contradictory answer to tattoo the witness as a pathological liar.

"To your knowledge, did you start with false oral statements to Sergeant Abraham?"

"I started to tell him the truth on some things." Atkinson tried to dodge the question.

"Have you lied about this case?"

"To some point."

"Now, you want the jury to believe you are telling the truth?" Barletta, his voice rising ever so slightly, sliced into the witness's veracity.

"That's right."

The prosecution next called Dr. Robert Macoskey. When the defense objected, Judge Balph ordered the testimony to be taken in camera, the legal term for a conversation outside the hearing of the jury, before ruling. During the questioning, Macoskey, a professor at Slippery Rock University, confirmed his credentials and discussed two schools of Satanism. One sect worships an external deity or power named Satan. Another branch focuses upon mankind's proclivity to do evil. Anton Szandor LaVey, high priest of the Church of Satan, espoused the second view as put forth in his book *The Satanic Bible*.

D.A. Williams argued the need to admit Dr. Macoskey's testimony as an expert witness to demonstrate, "The defendant's actions in influencing other people were consistent with believers of the satanic cult." The judge allowed the witness's appearance.

Dr. Macoskey explained LaVey's belief in the "satanic power resident in the human being." Under this doctrine, mankind is egocentric, inherently selfish and in opposition to everything the Judeo-Christian tradition represents. LaVey's followers support their ideology with ritual paraphernalia incorporating skulls, swords, black drapery and an altar.

When the D.A. showed photographs from Costal's apartment, Dr. Macoskey identified various items and the rituals associated with them.

"I show you Exhibit 140."

"What is on the wall is a mandola. It's a Hindu word for a circle. This mandola seems to have the signs and symbols of the zodiac. Astrology has played a very real role in occult practices."

"I show you Exhibit 141 and ask what is indicated about the occult?"

"The picture on the wall is one of the many representations of Satan. This one is interesting because it follows one of the traditional assumptions that Satan is a hermaphrodite."

"Will you elucidate?"

"The concept of dualism is a very old concept. Man very early discovered there were at least two sides to himself, so symbolism, tradition and literature are full of opposites: light and dark, good and bad, male and female." The witness continued, "There have always been people desirous of belonging to something, because of bad family backgrounds, or they think they have been punished by society. It's to those people that the group classified as satanic have made an appeal....Frequently the people who were involved were impressionable, were lonely and were willing to do anything to get support from others, no matter how aberrant the behavior might be."

"Now, there were four steps in the initiation process. The first of these was the initiate was asked to make public testimony that he was entering the cult of his own free will. Secondly, the initiate was asked to disavow his religion.

Hermaphrodite Satan at Costal apartment. *Courtesy of the New Castle Police Department.*

Thirdly, every individual made a compact with the superior deity. In many instances, this was understood to be Satan. The last part of the traditional initiation was the attachment of a permanent mark in some concealed spot. Tradition has it that there was a mark of Satan."

"There is a record of using drug and hallucinogens to prepare the initiate to participate in homosexual or humiliating acts. The idea was to push the initiate so far outside the bounds of normal morality that he could never come back."

"Would the inducing of the initiate to commit crimes fit into that category?" asked the D.A.

"Yes. There is a considerable record of murder, but also cannibalism, whereby it's necessary to eat the flesh of the individual murdered. I might mention a form of communion was quite typical. In gross terms, the wine of Christian communion was converted to either urine or menstrual blood, and the host was dried human feces. Now, a person who has the societal mentality I have described, whereby he's doing degrading acts, and you have the possibility of him being killed, then you have a rather solid routine to initiate then retain such people within the group."

"Now, I ask you is there any such thing as a curse involved in working on an initiate?"

"Oh yes, books and books of curses surrounded with all manner of symbolism and paraphernalia. Creating symbolically a person and sticking it with pins, burning it or putting it under water was called sympathetic magic and is attached to this as well."

"Is this kind of belief necessary?"

"Yes, every official satanic cult has a leader and customarily twelve followers. In other words, the appropriate number is thirteen. In witchcraft, this is called a coven," Dr. Macoskey explained, an aura of authority echoing through his voice.

"Can you aid us in giving the concept of power held over people in the coven?"

"The leader theoretically has absolute power, because he represents the divinity."

"Doctor, is there any evidence in the history of cultism that indicates cult members can be induced to commit acts that are not what other people would commit?"

"Yes. One clear example is Guyana. An individual managed to get nine hundred people to commit suicide."

Throughout Dr. Macoskey's dialogue, Costal avoided eye contact with either the witness or the jury. The allowed testimony caused irreparable damage to his case. As a guard escorted the manacled prisoner outside the jury's sight, from the courthouse to the Lawrence County Jail across the street at the end of the day's testimony, Costal conjured a silent curse to stop the know-it-all doctor and the district attorney.

By the time Frank Costal walked to the stand the next morning like a disciplined puppy, he recognized the jury had settled on his guilt. He spoke quietly and meekly and belittled Satanism by referring to his library of the occult as "goofy books."

Right: The demons Samael and Lilith. *Courtesy of the New Castle Police Department.*

Below: Exhibits 154 and 155 at the Costal trial, satanic books. *Courtesy of the New Castle Police Department.*

When Barletta asked if he played a hermaphrodite in a carnival, Costal answered with a toothless grin, "Played it good. I had lots of fun with the carnival."

Costal proved to be an easy target—his homosexuality, Satanism, bohemian lifestyle and weirdo friends sickened the conservative, rural jury. He failed to present an alibi, had difficulty remembering times and dates and claimed never to have met Larry Kadunce, nor had any knowledge of the crime. His testimony branded him as slow-witted and amoral.

During his closing argument, Bartletta sympathized with the jury's rage at the brutal slaying of Dawn and Kathy Kadunce. The attorney related that he had a three-year-old child, and the crime sickened him. However, the jury should aim its anger at the real murderer, not Costal.

"Now, my client is guilty. He's guilty of being a homosexual. My client is guilty of having been in the carnival. He's guilty of being slightly eccentric, of wearing a long beard and long hair. You might classify him as the original hippy of New Castle. He's guilty of shoplifting. He's guilty of having told people he was a devil worshiper. He's guilty of having had an apartment with plastic bats and wax skulls, an apartment that looked like Halloween all year...."

"The prosecutor has made a great deal out of the fact he was a homosexual, that he told people he was a devil worshiper. He painted a picture during the two weeks of presentation that this was a hideous monster. Now, when he took the stand, he did not have a pitchfork in his hands. He didn't have an eyeball in the center of his forehead."

The defense pointed out the faulty memory and conflicting statements of many of the state's witnesses. Even the police reports presented difficulties. One time Atkinson arrived in one car and another time in a different car. One time it was hot, another cold.

Barletta branded the state's star witness, Mike Atkinson, as a psychopath whose testimony should be discounted. The attorney suggested another potential suspect. "It's easy to say it was the husband, but we'll never know what happened in that house."

The defense pointed to his client and continued, "This is not a witch trial. This is a murder trial. The question is, did this man do it? I don't think Frank Costal did it. I don't think Frank Costal is that person."

The D.A. took in the summation, jotting notes in response to each and every point. Then, it was his turn, and he rose to make the best of it.

"You were told by Mr. Barletta that you will never know what happened. Some of those things we won't know maybe, and you don't need to know

Left: Frank Costal
testifying. *Courtesy of the
New Castle Police Department.*

Below: Frank Costal on the
stand. *Courtesy of the New
Castle Police Department.*

them." The D.A. explained that it was unnecessary to know whether Atkinson, Costal or the husband performed the actual killings. "They went there and killed these people and which one of them did the act, if they were acting in concert, doesn't make any difference. They're all guilty of murder. All of this evidence indicates there were more than one—two, maybe three, and he's one of them." Williams pointed his finger at the defendant. "The testimony of his own friends puts him there."

"For ten years in New Castle, he's talked to people telling he was a cultist, a devil worshiper, that he practiced these arts." The D.A. paused and stared at the defendant, shaking his head from side to side to demonstrate his disgust. "And then he gets up here and tells you it's all a joke. He didn't believe in it at all. It didn't work. We know the defendant is a liar. He's very deceitful."

"Dr. Macoskey says cult members are driven to do perverse things the ordinary person couldn't even conceive. He gave you an example. Jim Jones in Guyana. That's cultism. The American people would never have believed such things were possible if it weren't documented."

"You look at these photographs of that little girl and the diagram of the knife wounds. They are so heinous you couldn't believe that kind of thing would happen unless there was no way you could discount it. It's not explainable—except by followers of cults that have a regard for evil. Costal gets power from his rituals."

"This man had the power to get a psychopath like Mike Atkinson to go with him. He had the power to get Larry Kadunce to let him in the house without protecting his wife and daughter. Maybe he didn't know all the things that were going to happen."

Like Amos, the biblical prophet of doom, fired up with the light of righteousness, District Attorney Williams eyed the defendant and delivered a salvo from Proverbs, "'There's a way which unto a man seemeth right, but the end is the way to death.' It seems right that he should have Kathy Kadunce's husband as his lover. That he should have that girl punished for messing him up. When Mr. Costal took the stand, he talked lightheartedly, as if this devil worship is a joke—some joke!"

"Ben Clingensmith told you he had run the church down, said terrible things about the Lord, about Mary. Dr. Macoskey told you the satanic belief is the opposite of religion. We say God is good. They say he's bad. That's what Dr. Macoskey told you. The same idea came from his friend, Ben Clingensmith. Up at his house, Susan Garcia, one of them, his friend, comes forward as they all were, anti religion."

"We ask you to weigh all this, how his friends say he lived, what kinds of friends he had, who they were and the kinds of activities they were engaged in. He's an actor. He's been acting a long time, and he was acting here. We submit, ladies and gentlemen, that you do not accept that act. We ask that you convict this man of the murder of both of these people."

The silence in the courtroom presented the serenity of a Sunday morning church service as the D.A. completed his sermon. Not one of the men or women in the jury budged an iota. Neither the objections of Barletta nor the instructions of Judge Balph would sway the jury. Frank Costal's fate was preordained. After a three-and-a-half-hour deliberation, the jury of seven men and five women found him guilty of murder in the first degree on two counts.

Following the verdict reached at the conclusion of the fourteen-day trial, District Attorney Don Williams told the paper, "Anybody who holds the word of God in contempt is in for a lot of trouble." The Buckel family expressed their satisfaction with the guilty judgment.

Sergeant Abraham drank in the result of the trial with a combination of relief and elation. Although the pressure of the investigation oozed through his pores, he knew he had done a good job.

"Gig, this was like shooting ducks in a barrel. We had him the whole way, but you never know with a jury."

"One more to go, Babe. If we get Lou Kadunce, we will have a clean sweep of all the faggots," Gig answered, certain the husband would go down.

12

THE KADUNCE TRIAL

Sergeant Abraham anticipated an easy conviction of thirty-year-old Lou/Larry Kadunce. The case looked rock-solid. Just in case, Chuck patted his handcuffs for good luck. Soon, he would be able to put the double homicide and subsequent investigation behind him. But the future proved Abraham wrong.

During the formal arraignment, while Abraham concentrated on the information presented, the defendant clutched a paperback Bible between his hands. Kadunce sat emotionless as District Justice Howard Hanna set bond at $100,000, an amount far beyond his ability to pay.

At the start of the trial on Monday, January 11, 1982, New Castle's winter weather sat at a frigid fifteen degrees. Olivia Newton-John's song "Physical" led the pop-music charts. Stephen King's *Cujo* topped the country's best-seller book list. Ronald Reagan sat in the White House as president, and Angelo Sands served as mayor of the city.

Several factors complicated the state's opportunity for an easy conviction. Lou Kadunce presented a pleasing physical appearance in contrast to Mike Atkinson's menacing stare or Frank Costal's pockmarked and roughhewn face. Kadunce's demeanor calmed the jury. An array of normal-acting family and friends paraded to the stand to speak on his behalf.

The November elections brought a new Democratic district attorney. William Panella unseated incumbent Don Williams. Recognizing his former opponent's familiarity with the case, Panella offered Mr. Williams $10,000 to prosecute the trial. Williams declined. He had more than enough of the

Larry Kadunce returning from his trial. *Courtesy of the New Castle Police Department.*

Kadunce murder trials. Since Panella rarely litigated his own cases, preferring the organizational aspects of the job, he assigned the Commonwealth's case to Norman Barilla, a 1976 graduate of Ohio Northern Law School. Lacking Williams's extensive legal experience and knowledge of the case, Barilla also found himself short of time for adequate preparation.

This case itself was weaker than the prior two. The jury questioned both the quality of the witnesses and what could induce this soft-spoken husband to murder his daughter and wife. Finally, the court appointed Norman Levine, the son of a highly respected lawyer and a battler, to represent Kadunce, since Lou Pomerico found himself unable to try the case due to a conflict. Levine, a Case Western law school graduate, pegged the Commonwealth's key witness, Mike Atkinson, as a dull-witted, psychopathic liar. As the discrepancies between Atkinson's current testimony and his prior statements multiplied, his entire testimony came off as ludicrous and unbelievable.

Atkinson possessed limited reading skills. Attorney Levine exploited this weakness. After firing each question, he watched Atkinson squirm while reading his previous statements and then contradicting himself. The defense

Attorney Norman Levine. *Lawrence County Bar Association.*

attorney relished the looks of disbelief on the faces of the jury. He watched the panel move to his side as the thoroughly addled Atkinson drifted from one inconsistency to the next.

"Would you like to read your prior testimony to refresh your memory?"

"I don't need no help." Atkinson answered.

During his closing argument, Norman Levine, meticulously clad in a dark tailored suit and an upscale striped tie—so different from the more subtle and conservative clothing worn by his father, yet he was equally skillful as a litigator—stressed the state's failure to prove a motive, providing the jury discounted Atkinson's erratic testimony. Levine knew he didn't have to prove his client's innocence, merely raise a strong question mark.

"The prosecution has failed to establish my client's guilt beyond a reasonable doubt. I stand before you not to demonstrate my client's innocence. His innocence is already presumed. What possible motive could this man have for murdering his wife?" Levine lowered his voice and adjusted his glasses while registering the temper of the jury. "I suggest there isn't one. Mike Atkinson, chief witness for the prosecution, tells you he wanted drugs, so he ordered them from Frank Costal, and Frank Costal is going to get them from Lou Kadunce." The attorney pointed to his client. "Do you mean to tell me that if this man was selling drugs he wouldn't have excess money?" The attorney paused for effect. "He says he has to live from hand to mouth. He has to go on extra jobs, and we are supposed to believe this guy is in the sale of drugs." The attorney lowered his eyes and shook his head from side to side in disbelief.

"Homosexuality? Who did we hear that from? Mike Atkinson! I submit to you, ladies and gentlemen, this man doesn't like men. He likes women. I further submit the testimony in this trial has shown that by his brief encounter with Mary Akers."

"And lastly, jealousy. Lou killed his wife because he was jealous. I suggest this is facetious. What does Mary Akers say? She says, one, he is a gentle person; two, he treated me like a lady; three, he adored his daughter. There is absolutely no motive after you disregard economics, drugs, homosexuality and jealousy. There is little question that one of your chief considerations in this case will be whether you believe the testimony of Michael Atkinson. He is the only person who places Larry Kadunce at the scene of the murders. I can find at least fifteen discrepancies in his testimony." Levine cleared his throat.

"I suggest to you, ladies and gentlemen, this testimony is from a corrupt and polluted source and must be looked upon with disfavor. I ask you to look at the fact that since January of 1980, he has been catered to, that all he wanted was a deal for his father and he didn't want to be called a baby killer. He changed his story at his own trial and under oath told something completely different when he got another deal, which got him off the death penalty in another pending homicide, the Puz case."

"How can you possibly find Lawrence Kadunce guilty beyond a reasonable doubt after observing Atkinson on the witness stand, after hearing his testimony, after hearing what transpired prior to his testimony in Costal and subsequent to Costal? As I said previously, except for Mike Atkinson, there is no case against Lawrence Kadunce. I believe we have been able to explain his conduct as to his family, motive, cooperation, friends, tests and statements that all have been consistent. Now that the entire case has been laid before you, I think I am entitled to a verdict of not guilty, and, ladies and gentlemen, in returning this verdict, you will vindicate a principle of law that people are not tried by newspapers, not tried by rumor, but are tried by American jurors called to do justice and to decide upon the evidence. I ask you for, and I claim from you a verdict of not guilty."

Following a brief deliberation, the jury provided Levine and his client Lou Kadunce with the verdict of not guilty.

13

THE REST OF THE STORY

Did Mike Atkinson, Frank Costal and Lawrence Kadence receive proper justice? That is the question. Only God and the consciences of the guilty can be certain. Undoubtedly, Atkinson had taken part in the Dawn and Kathy Kadunce murders as well as that of Rosie Puz. A jury of his peers delivered a sentence of life imprisonment without parole. Could he have been involved in the Gargasz-Withers killings of 1975 or the murder of several missing persons? Quite possibly so.

A second jury convicted Frank Costal largely on Mike Atkinson's testimony. One might wonder if he had been a victim of a witch hunt, convicted due to his Satanism, homosexuality, carnival background and bohemian lifestyle rather than on actual evidence.

A third jury rejected star witness Mike Atkinson's veracity and freed Lawrence Kadunce. Following his release from jail, Kadunce established a new life for himself, remarrying in 1984 and moving away from New Castle.

Frank Costal served a life sentence at Western Penitentiary in Pittsburgh. When I visited him, he asked me for copies of his trial transcripts, and I provided them. He claimed never to have met Larry Kadunce and had no first-hand knowledge of the murders. Likewise, Kadunce had told the police that he never met Costal.

Costal joked about his prison job producing license plates, "I made one saying you get a good screwing in Pennsylvania," rather than "You've got a friend in Pennsylvania." Although bitter about his interment, he coped well, painting during his free time. He seemed popular with the other inmates and acted less despondently than one might think.

Left: Frank Costal at Western Penitentiary with the author. *Author's collection.*

Below: Huntington Prison. *Author's collection.*

Frank G. Costal Jr.
P.O. Box 99901
Pittsburgh, Pa. 15233

2 April 1990

Dear Mr. Perelman

Let me begin this letter by extending you my best wishes for the upcoming Holiday Season. May you achieve success in all of your endeavors.

For the last several months I have been fighting an uphill battle to have your name placed back on my visiting list, and finally it has been done. I would like to speak with you as soon as possible because there has been a lot happening recently in my case. I have recieved several visits, and two in particular, I believe you will be very intrested in. To date I have not recieved any of the notes of testimony other than the ones you have sent, but, as you know, I have several alternative routes that I have at my disposal, but thing are proceeding in an orderly fashion.

In closing I would like to express my sincere wish in seeing you as soon as possib le, because as I said there has been several revelations in my case. thank you , and I hope to see you soon

Respectfully

Frank G. Costal Jr.
AP-6710

cc/file

Letter from Frank Costal to the author. *Author's collection.*

"On the balance, I haven't too many regrets. Life could have been worse," he confided. Since my last visit, he deteriorated, suffering a mental breakdown. The authorities transferred him to the psychological ward, where the seventy-one-year-old prisoner died in December 1999.

Michael Atkinson served his life sentence at Pennsylvania's Huntington Prison, where he became a constant thorn to the guards. The warden described him as one of his worst prisoners.

Members of the New Castle police had a suspicion that Atkinson might have taken part in at least two missing-person murders in addition to the Puz and Kadunce killings. Melanie Meachen, a relative of the Gargasz family,

Western Penitentiary.
Author's collection.

and the state police believed Atkinson had been involved in the unsolved Gargasz-Withers murders of 1975 as well. Melanie spent many hours researching my police and trial notes looking for answers.

Hard time, illness and a demented brain beat down Atkinson, gutting him into a mere shadow of the terror he once had been. New teeth, a stroke, a heart bypass and embolism surgery cost the taxpayers tens of thousands of dollars but left the prisoner with slurred speech and difficulty communicating.

During a visit to Huntington Prison with officers Gagliardo and Abraham to question Atkinson about a missing person and possible murder victim, the manacled and barely understandable prisoner sat sullenly at a table. The police seated me next to Atkinson. I couldn't help but notice that each man wrapped a leg around the bolted-down chairs for support. Gig later claimed he did it "because I thought Mike might charge me or Chuck. He didn't know you."

Mike claimed Leona Bullock, an ex-girlfriend and the mother of his third child, committed the Kadunce killings. He swore neither he nor Costal had anything to do with the Kadunce murders, remaining unrepentant and claiming innocence to the end. Atkinson died in 2013.

POSTSCRIPT

Many of the key actors in this story are dead. Charles Abraham, who became chief of police in 1994 and later a district justice, succumbed to a heart attack at age fifty-six in 1999. Lieutenant Frank Gagliardo remained as head of the detective bureau until his retirement. He died from prostate cancer in 2014 at age eighty-one. Norman Levine expired in 2005 at age fifty-nine and Judge William Balph in 1992 at age sixty-one, both from heart attacks. District Attorney Donald Williams, a one-time chair of the Lawrence County Republican Party, died in 2001 at age seventy-eight. Rose Butera (Sanchez) died in 2001 at age fifty-eight. One of her daughters, Jonilyn Young, was stabbed and murdered in 1989. The police have yet to solve the crime.

ABOUT THE AUTHOR

Dale Richard Perelman, a native of New Castle, Pennsylvania, has written: *Mountain of Light: The Story of the Koh-I-Noor Diamond*; *The Regent: The Story of the Regent Diamond*; *Centenarians: One Hundred 100-Year-Olds Who Made a Difference*; *Steel: The Story of Pittsburgh's Iron and Steel Industry, 1852–1902*; *Road To Rust, the Disintegration of the Steel Industry in Western Pennsylvania and Eastern Ohio*; *Lessons My Father Taught Me* and *The Scottish Rite Cathedral* (coauthored with Rob Cummings.) Perelman holds a Bachelor of Arts degree from Brown University in English literature, an MBA in industrial relations from the Wharton School of the University of Pennsylvania, a graduate gemologist's designation from the Gemological Institute of America and a certificate of completion from the Yale University summer writer's program.